Children of Alcoholics: A Guidebook for Educators, Therapists, and Parents

Second Edition

Robert J. Ackerman
Indiana University of Pennsylvania

Learning Publications, Inc.
Holmes Beach, Florida

Library of Congress Card Number: 78-55067

Learning Publications, Inc.
P.O. Box 1326
Holmes Beach, Florida 33509

Hardcover ISBN 0-918452-50-3
Softcover ISBN 0-918452-47-3

Cover Design by Rob Gutek

Printing: 1 2 3 4 5 6 7 8   Year: 3 4 5 6 7 8
Printed and bound in the United States of America

to
Kimberly and Jason
the verbs in my life

ACKNOWLEDGEMENTS

I wish to thank all the children of alcoholics, young and old, who shared themselves with me. I am grateful for the many insights and candid conversations. I hope that together we will make the way easier for those who follow.

To my friend for all seasons, Edsel L. Erickson, who has pushed, pulled and praised from the first edition to this second edition, thank you.

Additionally, I would like to thank Rebecca S. Lauffner for her tremendous assistance in updating the appendices and Candie S. Stewart for her administrative support. Your time and efforts are much appreciated.

TABLE OF CONTENTS

PART A

THE CHILD OF AN ALCOHOLIC: WHAT IT'S LIKE

1

Now You See Them, Now You Don't

More than ten percent of the population of the United States is being raised or was raised in an alcoholic home. It is commonly agreed that there are between twenty-five and twenty-eight million children of alcoholics in our society. But where are they? How can millions of people, regardless of age, be virtually invisible, undetected and ignored? Several factors contribute to this dilemma.

First, although alcoholism has existed for thousands of years we are just beginning to understand, accept and assist alcoholics. It is estimated that there are 9.3 to 10 million alcoholics currently in this country (NIAAA, 1980). It is only recently that we have begun to assess the magnitude of alcoholism and the problems of being an alcoholic. In many respects, we are still "centered" on the problems of only the alcoholic and do not consider the impact of alcoholism on others, especially on the children of alcoholics. It is almost as if we are just "discovering" that along with the existence of generations of alcoholism we have also had generations of children of alcoholics.

A second contributing factor has been the concept of alcoholism itself and ideas about the "typical" alcoholic. It has only been in the last thirty years that we have begun to accept and understand alcoholism as a disease. We have been hesitant to accept alcoholism as a disease and not a moral or deviancy problem. This hesitancy contributed to not only ignoring the alcoholic, but also his or her family. An additional complication has been our tendency to stereotype alcoholism as being "skid row" even though only 3-5% of alcoholics fit in this category. In fact, approximately seventy percent of so-called "average" alcoholics are men and women with a good home, job and family (NIAAA, 1980). Alcoholics are, in reality, our neighbors, our friends and the parents of children.

Third, children of alcoholics themselves have contributed to their being unnoticed. Because of the societal uncertainty surrounding alcoholism, most children of alcoholics have not openly shared their experiences or received help. For many children of alcoholics, more effort has gone into covering up the alcoholism than into seeking help. In fact, only five percent of children of alcoholics are in treatment specifically for those problems that arise from being a child of an alcoholic. Many children of alcoholics are being noticed outside the family, but not for the direct effects of alcoholism. Unfortunately, estimates indicate that as high as twenty percent of the caseloads of juvenile courts and child guidance clinics are children who come from alcoholic homes. In these situations, the children are being seen for problems other than for being the child of an alcoholic. Often the family alcoholism is not taken into consideration by others or is hidden by the child.

All of these variables have resulted in a variety of problems for children of alcoholics. These problems are emotional, developmental, physiological and social. However, before any of these problems can be addressed, the foremost problem for the majority of children of alcoholics must be overcome. This problem is that the needs of children of alcoholics are not recognized. If the child of the alcoholic is "invisible," his or her problems are also invisible. Not only does this situation often exist in our society, but also in the alcoholic family itself. In homes with an alcoholic parent, even though all family members are affected, not all members are considered since the alcoholic is the center of attention. Often those remembered last are the children.

ALCOHOLISM AND THE FAMILY

Living with an alcoholic is a family affair. Because it subjects all members of a household to constant stress and fears of various kinds, it has often been referred to as a "family illness." To one degree or another, all members of the family are affected. However, not all alcoholic families nor all members of the same family are affected in a similar manner.

The Collective Mind

Not all alcoholic families nor all members of the family are affected in the same way. To assume that all family members are equally and identically affected is to assume that the family possesses a "collective mind." The "collective mind" assumes that the entire family shares the same feelings about the alcoholic and alcoholism. Additionally, this would mean that all alcoholic families are alike. This is not true. To understand the effects of alcoholism on the family, we need to look at the individual members of the family. The individual is the beginning unit of analysis to understanding family dynamics in an alcoholic home. This is true for the alcoholic as well as the nonalcoholic family members.

Why are individual members of the alcoholic family affected differently? To answer this question, three variables should be considered. These are the degree of alcoholism, the type of alcoholic in the home, and the individual perception of potential harm from living with an alcoholic.

The *degree* of alcoholism refers to the severity of the problem. How often does the drinking occur? Is the alcoholic a binge drinker once a month, intoxicated daily, or totally unpredictable? Can the alcoholic be relied upon to function socially and for performance of his or her normal duties? Is the alcoholic employed or capable of working in and outside the home?

Closely related to the degree of alcoholism is the *type* of alcoholic that lives with the family. One type of alcoholic is the belligerent type who is verbally abusive and is consistently looking for an argument. The recipient of these attacks is exposed to high degrees of verbal and emotional abuse.

Another type of alcoholic may be jovial after drinking. This person likes to laugh a lot and is preoccupied with entertaining. Being around this alcoholic, although not physically or verbally harmful, may be emotionally stressful due to inappropriate joking or the inability to express himself or herself seriously.

These are a few examples of the many different types of alcoholics. Obviously these differences can be manifested in a variety of forms for nonalcoholic family members. A child growing up with a physically abusive alcoholic parent may have a very different perspective on alcoholism as opposed to a child living with a highly passive alcoholic.

The variables of *degree* and *type* relate to the alcoholic. The third variable—and perhaps the most important for nonalcoholic family members—is their *perception* of the situation.

Does the nonalcoholic family member perceive the situation as harmful? Often our perception dictates our reactions. Whatever we perceive to be real, we react to it as if it is. Reality may be secondary to perception. In an alcoholic home, some nonalcoholic members may feel minimally affected because they perceive that the alcoholism is not harmful to them. However, in the same family others may be totally devastated because they feel that they are living in a crisis situation.

In summary, although we are concerned with alcoholism in the family, we need to be even more concerned with the effects of alcoholism on the individual members of a family. Each family member requires his or her own individual analysis of the situation. To understand the individual situation, the degree of alcoholism, the type of alcoholic in the family and the nonalcoholic's individual perceptions must be considered.

Which Parent is Addicted

Do we have a higher probability that the father is alcoholic or that the mother is alcoholic in a family? To answer this question, we must consider several factors.

In our society today, if a woman is married to a male alcoholic and there are children under the age of eighteen in the family, nine out of ten women will stay with the alcoholic. However, if the situation is reversed, and she is the alcoholic, only one out of ten males will stay. Many of the women's reasons for staying range from a lack of viable alternatives to denial. Additionally, the norms of society must be considered. For example, a male can become inebriated and engage in drunken behavior and still be permitted to feel masculine. It is difficult for a woman to become inebriated and engage in drunken behavior and feel feminine. For the male, there exists a complementary norm of excessive drinking and masculinity. However, for the female there exists a conflicting norm regarding excessive drinking and femininity. Where a complementary norm exists, there is a higher probability of its continual occurrence and a higher level of societal acceptance.

Another factor may be that if a woman has children and she is suspected of having a drinking problem, one of the first things that may be said about her is that she is an "unfit" mother. It is unlikely that the male will stay in this situation. However, how long does male alcoholism continue before we hear that he is an "unfit" father? The woman has traditionally remained in this situation.

Finally, there simply are a greater number of male alcoholics than female alcoholics in our society. Some estimates indicate that seventy-six percent of problem drinkers are men and only twenty-four percent are women (NIAAA, 1980). Although we are currently discovering female alcoholics at a faster rate than male alcoholics, it is doubtful that given societal values and socialization patterns, alcoholism will become an "equal opportunity" destroyer (Ackerman, 1978).

In summary, if the alcoholic family is physically residing in the same house, there is a higher probability that the alcoholic in the family is the father. The percentage of cases where both spouses are alcoholics represents only twenty percent of the alcoholic homes in America. The majority of alcoholic homes, therefore, have a higher probability of only one spouse being alcoholic, and this spouse is usually the father.

FAMILY RESPONSES TO THE ALCOHOLIC PARENT

Responses to alcoholism in the family can be divided into four phases. These are called reactive, active, alternative and family unity phases. These different periods are distinguished by several characteristics which dominate the particular phase. However, not all alcoholic families experience these

conditions similarly nor are these phases universally progressive. That is, not all families will progress from one phase
to the next. Many families unfortunately remain in the first
phase and never reach the fourth state of sobriety and family
growth.

Phase I — The Reactive Phase

The reactive phase is consistently dominated by the behavior of nonalcoholic family members reacting to the
alcoholic's behavior. During this time most family members
become extremely cautious in their behavior in order to avoid
or to further complicate the existing problems of alcoholism.
However, by being reactive they are constantly adapting their
behavior in order to minimize or survive an unhealthy
situation. Much of this adaptation will not only have detrimental effects on those who are adjusting, but also it
indirectly allows and supports the continuing alcoholism.
During the reactive phase three typical family characteristics
emerge. These are family denial, coping strategies and social
disengagement.

Family Denial

It is ironic that family members deny a drinking problem in their family because this is exactly what the alcoholic does. We know that, for the alcoholic, denial is functional for the continuation of drinking. As long as the alcoholic denies that he or she has a problem, there is no reason to seek a solution. Nonalcoholic family members also deny, but their denial is totally dysfunctional to meeting their needs. Everyone in the family denies that anything is wrong, yet no one feels right.

Family denial of alcoholism occurs in at least three ways: systemic denial, protection versus exposure and the primary patient philosophy.

Systemic Denial

Systemic denial means that the entire system denies the existence of a problem. Certainly the family is analogous to a system which is a pattern of interrelationships. Within the family system, denial usually occurs when family members do not want to admit that one of them is an alcoholic or because they perceive alcoholism as some sort of reflection upon themselves. This is particularly true in the case of non-alcoholic spouses who are women. For example, in American society, if the husband has a drinking problem often there is a connotation that the wife is partly responsible. Statements such as "she drove him to drink" are typical. Even though these statements are not empirically correct, the woman may perceive them as true, and that she may be responsible for his development of alcoholism. Therefore, as long as she denies that her husband has a drinking problem, she simultaneously denies that she has anything to do with causing the problem.

An additional form of systemic denial occurs at the societal level. The family itself is also part of a larger system, which is the community or society in which it resides. Our society does not readily admit to alcohol problems. Although we accept alcoholism as a disease, there remain many who attach a moral stigma or deviancy status to alcoholism. Consequently, we cannot blame a family for covering up a condition that is not understood by society.

Another consideration is that the family is in an unfortunate position of "negative anonymity." That is, being anonymous has negative implications for the family. They are in a no win situation. To deny on the one hand keeps others from knowing or judging, but on the other hand it keeps the family from getting help. This situation is similar to the alcoholic who covers up his or her drinking, but it is also different if getting help is considered. For example, for the alcoholic who wants help, he or she may join Alcoholics Anonymous. In this instance, their anonymity works for them. For the nonalcoholic family member, however, their anonymity works against them. One of the paramount problems for families of alcoholics is being recognized as individuals in need of assistance. If they are to overcome denial, they must overcome anonymity.

Protection vs. Exposure

A second form of family denial is protection versus exposure. Protection means not talking about the problem as a method of sheltering one from the situation. Exposure means not just experiencing the problem, but recognizing it, discussing it, and overcoming any effects. In the alcoholic home, particularly with children, the nonalcoholic spouse will often attempt to protect the children. A common mode of protection is to treat the situation as if it does not exist. This is impossible in an alcoholic home. However, it is not uncommon for the nonalcoholic parent to say "I have to cover up because I want to protect my children." Usually this means that the situation is never discussed, particularly with the children. This would be fine if protection was the problem, but it is not. Exposure to alcoholism is the problem. Trying to protect someone when they are exposed is a form of denial. In essence, the exposure is denied, any effects from the exposure, and more importantly, the need for help is denied. If we are going to help nonalcoholic family members, we need to concentrate our efforts not on protection, but in overcoming the effects from exposure. To assume that children in an alcoholic home do not know and feel the effects of alcoholism is naive. They know. They may not understand, but they know. Living in an alcoholic home is not a "spectator sport." All are involved to one degree or another, including the passive participants. This cannot be denied away.

Primary Patient Philosophy

The third form of denial is the "primary patient philosophy." In the past when alcoholism existed in a family, it was assumed that the alcoholic was the primary concern. The alcoholic was to be helped first. However, the majority of alcoholics do not quit drinking, and while we are waiting for sobriety to occur, families fall apart, marriages may collapse, and children grow up and leave home. As long as we consider the alcoholic the primary concern, we again deny intervention for nonalcoholic family members. Nonalcoholic family members should be considered the primary interests and not the alcoholic. This is not to ignore the alcoholic, but to insure that we do not ignore the effects of alcoholism on the family while drinking is occurring. Additionally, as mentioned earlier, there are far more nonalcoholic family members than alcoholics, and their needs cannot be denied.

Coping Strategies

The key to surviving an alcoholic home is adaptation. You learn to adapt your behavior in order to minimize the effects of alcoholism. A method of adaptation is to develop coping strategies. In the alcoholic home, these strategies are developed even though the family denies the existence of alcoholism. The denial, however, in the home is no longer as strong, but it is maintained outside of the household. For this reason, coping strategies are "home remedies." They are efforts by nonalcoholic families to survive a situation while denying its existence to others. These strategies are severely limited, therefore, and seldom work. Coping strategies can be either verbal or behavioral attempts. At best they provide a brief, but anxious respite.

Verbal Coping Strategies

Verbal strategies are efforts by nonalcoholic family members to effectively communicate with the alcoholic about alcoholism. However, these efforts are usually interpreted by the alcoholic as "nagging" or persecution. As a response, the nonalcoholic resorts to morality lectures, pleas for self-respect, threats, promises, and statements such as "how could you do this to us?" Unfortunately most verbal strategies do little to motivate the alcoholic, but do a lot to raise anxiety.

However, verbal communication between nonalcoholic family members may be helpful. In most homes, no one wants to talk about the addiction; hoping the silence means non-existence. It is true that the problem cannot be talked away, but discussing verbally and sharing the "family secret" is a positive beginning for nonalcoholic family members in their attempts for recovery. Family members often develop verbal strategies in only one direction which is from the nonalcoholic to the alcoholic. Thus there is no possible positive reciprocal effect for them. Verbal interaction among nonalcoholic family members is a strategy available if they are willing to risk the sharing of information and feelings with each other.

Behavioral Coping Strategies

The second type of coping strategy is behavioral. The behavioral strategies are behaviors that nonalcoholic families knowingly or unknowingly adopt to cope with their situation. Typical behavior strategies are hiding alcohol, refusing to buy alcohol, marking bottles, avoiding the alcoholic or family members, staying away from home, and isolating oneself. Many families deny that they have developed coping strategies. However, it is difficult to deny their unusual behavior. In a home where drinking is permitted and is within normal acceptable limits, family members do not engage in this unusual behavior. Where drinking is abnormal, there exists abnormal nonalcoholic behavior as coping mechanisms. As a result of these coping strategies, nonalcoholic family members become socially disengaged from friends, family, community, and themselves.

As stated earlier, many nonalcoholic family members deny or are unaware of their participation in coping strategies. The following questionnaire has been developed for nonalcoholic family members to help to overcome their denial of the effects of alcoholism on their lives. Noteworthy is that most of these questions pertain to the behavior of nonalcoholic family members.

These questions should be answered by family members with as much honesty as possible. The questions were developed by Betty Reddy, Program Specialist, Alcoholism Treatment Center, Lutheran General Hospital, Park Ridge, Illinois.

1. Do you lose sleep because of a problem drinker?

2. Do most of your thoughts revolve around the problem drinker or problems that arise because of him or her?

3. Do you exact promises about the drinking which are not kept?

4. Do you make threats or decisions and not follow through on them?

5. Has your attitude changed toward this problem drinker (alternating between love and hate)?

6. Do you mark, hide, dilute and/or empty bottles of liquor or medication?

7. Do you think that everything would be O.K., if only the problem drinker would stop or control the drinking?

8. Do you feel alone, fearful, anxious, angry and frustrated most of the time? Are you beginning to feel dislike for yourself and to wonder about your sanity?

9. Do you find your moods fluctuating wildly as a direct result of the problem drinker's moods and actions?

10. Do you feel responsible and guilty about the drinking problem?

11. Do you try to conceal, deny, or protect the problem drinker?

12. Have you withdrawn from outside activities and friends because of embarrassment and shame over the drinking problem?

13. Have you taken over many chores and duties that you would normally expect the problem drinker to assume— or that were formerly his or hers?

14. Do you feel forced to try to exert tight control over the family expenditures with less and less success—and are financial problems increasing?

15. Do you feel the need to justify your actions and attitudes and, at the same time, feel somewhat smug and self-righteous compared to the drinker?

16. If there are children in the house, do they often take sides with either the problem drinker or the spouse?

17. Are the children showing signs of emotional stress, such as withdrawing, having trouble with authority figures, rebelling, acting-out sexually?

18. Have you noticed physical symptoms in yourself, such as nausea, a "knot" in the stomach, ulcers, shakiness, sweating palms, bitten fingernails?

19. Do you feel utterly defeated—that nothing you say or do will move the problem drinker? Do you believe that he or she can't get better?

20. Where this applies, is your sexual relationship with a problem drinker affected by feelings of revulsion; do you "use" sex to manipulate—or refuse sex to punish him or her?

Here are some additional questions specifically for children of alcoholics to help to assess their feelings about parental alcoholism (Brooks, 1981).

1. Do you worry about your mom's or dad's drinking?

2. Do you sometimes feel that you are the reason your parent drinks so much?

3. Are you ashamed to have your friends come to your house and are you finding more and more excuses to stay away from home?

4. Do you sometimes feel that you hate your parents when they are drinking and then feel guilty for hating them?

5. Have you been watching how much your parent drinks?

6. Do you try to make your parents happy so they won't get upset and drink more?

7. Do you feel you can't talk about the drinking in your home—or even how you feel inside?

8. Do you sometimes drink or take drugs to forget about things at home?

9. Do you feel if your parents really loved you they wouldn't drink so much?

10. Do you sometimes wish you had never been born?

11. Do you want to start feeling better?

Social Disengagements

Social disengagement is the withdrawing of family members from interaction with others. The family literally denies itself the support structure that it needs. This withdrawal is exacerbated.because the family feels that it must protect itself, has been embarrassed, or fears future encounters with others where the alcoholic is present. The family becomes isolated. At this point, families feel that there is a lack of available alternatives. The home becomes a "habit cage." However, families of alcoholics do not need to be isolated if they do not choose to be. Most families, however, rarely feel that they have a choice. They see their only response as withdrawal. This social disengagement can occur in two ways, physical and emotional withdrawal.

Physical Disengagement

Physical disengagement occurs when the family stops receiving and giving invitations for social interaction. The family is physically pulled back from contact with others. Children, for example, no longer invite their friends to their homes. Nonalcoholic spouses hide invitations to functions involving alcohol to avoid any confrontations or embarrassment. Fewer people stop by to visit because of the unpleasantness or tension from a previous visit. The family becomes significantly separated as a unit from others. This physical isolation can lead to emotional disengagement.

Emotional Disengagement

Emotional disengagement is a decline in positive emotional relationships. In the alcoholic home, this decline is replaced with an increase in negative emotions. The longer the alcoholism continues and the more the family withdraws, the greater the probability of negative emotions such as tension, anxiety, despair and powerlessness emerging.

A method of handling these negative emotions is to attempt to become "nonfeeling." That is, to deny and minimize negative feelings to prevent further pain. Thus avoidance becomes the norm for handling negative emotions. However, avoidance can lead to the denial of benefits of positive relationships which could be offsetting factors for the negative ones. The goals of positive relationships are sacrificed for the "comfortableness" of isolation within the family. However, as stated earlier, not all family members are affected equally. Some members are able to overcome the internal negative emotions by outside nonfamily relationships. In research with children of alcoholics, it was found that children who were able to establish primary relationships outside the home were not as likely to become alcoholic in their adult lives as children who did not establish these relationships (Ackerman, 1978). This is particularly relevant considering that approximately fifty percent of alcoholics come from an alcoholic home.

Of all the problems encountered by nonalcoholic family members, emotional isolation may be the greatest. It affects not only the nonalcoholic life within the family, but also outside the family. Healthy relationships are denied or postponed to survive an unhealthy situation. Most nonalcoholic family members do not assess the negative impact of this approach. They do what they believe makes the most sense at the time. The real impact may be found outside the family or for children in their adult lives. This is particularly true when considering that the children of alcoholics are disporportionately represented in juvenile courts, family courts, spouse and child abuse cases, divorce, within populations and plagued with psychological or emotional problems as adults.

Unfortunately many families of alcoholics do not go beyond the reactive phase. They either deny that the problem drinker is alcoholic, they helplessly hope for recovery, or they passively participate in the alcoholism syndrome. Thus stagnation at the reactive phase is likely to lead to these common effects on the alcoholic, the nonalcoholic spouse and the children (Coates, 1979).

The alcoholic:

- Denies the alcohol problem, blames others, forgets and tells stories to defend and protest against humiliation, attack, and criticism from others in the family

- Spends money for day-to-day needs on alcohol

- Becomes unpredictable and impulsive in behavior

- Resorts to verbal and physical abuse in place of honest open talk

- Loses trust of family, relatives, and friends

- Experiences diminishing sexual drive

- Has feeling of despair and hopelessness

- Thinks about suicide and possibly will make an attempt

● Shows deterioration of physical health.

The spouse:

● Often tries to hide and deny the existing problem of the alcoholic

● Takes on the responsibilities of the other person, carrying the load of two and perpetrating the spouse dependence

● Takes a job to get away from the problem and/or maintain financial security

● Finds it difficult to be open and honest because of resentment, anger, and hurt feelings

● Avoids sexual contact

● May over-protect the children, neglect them, and/or use them for emotional support

● Shows gradual social withdrawal and isolation

● May lose feelings of self-respect and self-worth

- May use alcohol or prescription drugs in an effort to cope.

The children:

- May be victims of birth defects

- May be torn between parents; in being loyal to one, they arouse and feel the anger of the other

- May be deprived of emotional and physical support

- Avoid peer activities, especially in the home out of fear and shame

- Learn destructive and negative ways of dealing with problems and getting attention

- Lack trust in anyone

- May lose sight of values, standards and goals because of the absence of consistent, strong parenting

- Suffer a diminishing sense of self-worth as a significant member of the family

II — The Active Phase

The main difference between the active and reactive phases is the responses of the nonalcoholic family member even though the alcoholic is still drinking. Rather than being passive to the effects on themselves from alcoholism they begin to take an active interest in themselves. No longer do they perceive themselves as totally under the alcoholic's control and they attempt to gain some control over their own lives. In this manner the family begins to "de-center" itself from alcoholism. In addition, family denial of alcoholism is not as strong. A major step into the active phase is the overcoming of denial by family members. They begin to realize that the problem cannot be denied away. Likewise, they are willing to abandon their anonymity in exchange for help and a viable alternative to how they have been existing. The two predominate characteristics of the active phase are *awareness* and *being normal.*

Awareness

During the active phase, the family develops a growing awareness about alcoholism, their family and themselves. Some of the awarenesses that develop are:

- they are not responsible for causing the alcoholism

- they do not have to live like this, that alternatives are available

- they recognize the need for help

- they realize that help is available

- they are not alone and do not have to be alone.

Much of this active time for nonalcoholic family members is becoming involved in their own recovery. They begin to become involved in various educational, counseling and self-help groups that are available to them. Hopefully during this time they realize that they too are important and that even though the alcoholic does not stop drinking that this does not necessarily stop them from getting help. During the reactive phase it may have been assumed that nothing could be done until the alcoholic received help. Now in the active phase they realize that to wait may be futile, denies their own needs and only continues and reinforces the impact of alcoholism on their lives.

Being Normal

During this period the nonalcoholic family members and particularly the nonalcoholic spouse attempts to stabilize the alcoholic home. Despite active alcoholism, i.e. the alcoholic is still drinking, it is decided to "get on with" normal family activities as much as possible. Even though it is desirable for the alcoholic to quit drinking and become a part of the normalizing process, sobriety is not a prerequisite. True it will impede the process, but what is actually happening during the normal stage is an open and honest attempt to make the best of a negative situation inside and outside of the home in order to overcome negative impacts of alcoholism. The idea that families can begin their recovery process and become involved in normal activities that were once avoided begins to take hold.

These activities may include supporting children to become involved in school and group activities, joining self-help groups, encouraging family conversations and the sharing of feelings. It also means that these endeavors do not necessarily pertain to alcoholism and recovery, but also and perhaps more importantly that they pertain to the normal activities of children who are not in alcoholic homes. These "other" activities have their benefits in not only the activities themselves, but also in the separation from alcoholism. These can serve as positive outside offsetting factors to a negative home environment as well as contribute to building better family interaction patterns.

Again, paramount to this phase is overcoming denial, risking the loss of anonymity and once again taking an active interest in their lives by the nonalcoholic family members. These steps begin with awareness of and a desire to feel normal.

III — The Alternative Phase

The alternative phase begins when all else has failed. The family now faces the painful question of whether or not separation is the viable alternative to survive alcoholism. It is not necessary that a family progress through both of the two previous phases. Some families will go directly from phase one into the alternative phase, while others will attempt the active phase before making the decision to separate. The characteristics of the alternative phase are *polarization, separation, change* and *family re-organization.*

Polarization

Prior to separation many alcoholic families go through a process of polarization. That is family members begin to withdraw from each other and are often forced into "choosing sides." Parents may begin to make threats to each other or statements to the children that they are considering a legal separation or divorce. For the children this means many things, but ultimately it means that they will not be living with both parents. The effects of alcoholism on their lives will now become even greater. It has now lead to a divorce. Unfortunately, alcoholism contributes to approximately forty percent of family court cases and thus many children of alcoholics experience the "double jeopardy" of being not only children of alcoholics, but also children of divorce.

Polarization is also the process leading up to a separation. In many cases this time of decision is long and painful and in some cases may be more traumatic than the actual separation. For children it is a time of impending change and is often accompanied with feelings of confusion, torn loyalties, fear, resentment, anger and increased isolation.

Separation

For some families the only viable alternative left to them will be family separation. For others, the separation will only compound existing problems. And still for others, they will exchange one set of problems for a new set of problems. In short, for some life will get better, for others it will be about the same and for others it will get worse. For many children separation will be life without daily contact with the alcoholic. However, even within the same family, this change may be greeted with different feelings. For younger children the loss of the parental role is of more concern than the loss of the alcoholic and for older children it may be the opposite. They may perceive that although they may be losing the parental role, that for all intents and purposes it was lost anyhow, and that they will no longer be affected by all of the family alcoholic problems. Much of this will be dependent upon how the family members perceive this change in their lives.

Change

There is a myth that change is in and of itself always traumatic. However, what should be considered when assessing the impact of change are the rates and the directions of change. That is, if the rate of change occurs too rapidly it can be traumatic due to the inability to adjust quickly enough. On the other hand, change that occurs too slowly can also be anxiety producing. For example, not only may separation be painful, but also the manner by which the separation has occurred can be significant. In some alcoholic families the process of polarization may have been a long and tedious affair while in other families polarization occurred too rapidly and the decision to separate was made in haste. On the other hand, however, it may be that the family members perceived that it was time for a much needed change and that the time was now. Thus the rate of change can help or hinder the alternative phase.

Additionally, the direction of change becomes critical for each family member. Individual family members see the new change to their advantage or disadvantage. If a child perceives that he or she will be worse off after separation then the change is likely to be seen as undesirable. Thus the child is against the change. However, if a child perceives that his or her life will improve, then the change is not problematic. Life without the alcoholic is seen as better than life with the alcoholic. In reality, for some members of the alcoholic family this will be true, for others it will not. Much depends upon how the new family grows and is re-organized.

Family Re-organization

For those alcoholic families that have chosen the alternative phase, several things can occur when re-organization takes place. The family begins to re-organize, pull together and grow. In these families, family members may begin to seek help for themselves or become further involved in their recovery process. Family members will begin to feel good about themselves, and establish healthy relationships within and outside of their family.

However, for some families re-organization will involve new and additional roles. The custodial spouse now faces the single parent role alone, whereas in the past even though the alcoholic parent was often absent at times, they helped in parenting. In addition, children may find themselves in roles with added responsibilities. All of the family members' new roles can, however, be impeded by old feelings and behaviors, such as, their feelings about alcoholism, being the child or the spouse of an alcoholic, resentment, anger, guilt, abandonment, failure and doubt. These feelings can be coupled with the old behaviors of consistently talking about the alcoholic, blaming problems on alcoholism, or holding the alcoholic solely responsible for their lives.

Re-organization can be further complicated by the recurring visits of the alcoholic parent, particularly if the alcoholic is still drinking. For example, the alcoholic can use the children to "get at" the nonalcoholic spouse. The children may become pawns between the spouses. This can be further complicated by the alcoholic seeking support from the children for a reconciliation. However, it is possible that within the same family, this idea can receive mixed reactions. Younger children, again, may favor the idea more than the older children because they may not have been exposed to the longevity of the alcoholism.

One of the main problems of re-organization will be the tendency to fall back into many of the patterns of the reactive phase. A family will need to be supported during the alternative phase if the alternatives are to become viable solutions.

IV — Family Unity Plan

Unfortunately, many alcoholic families never reach the family unity phase due to continuing alcoholism. There are no definitive progressive patterns to reach the unity phase. Some families will proceed directly from phase one to phase four, others will go through the first two phases and then to four, and still others may go through all the phases on their way to family unity. However, when they arrive, the family will face at least three characteristics of this phase which are sobriety, the "dry drunk," and family growth.

Sobriety

Central to the family unity phase is the maintaining of sobriety by the alcoholic. However, sobriety alone may not be enough. Certainly, it is superior to inebriation, but acceptance of the sober alcoholic back into the mainstream of the family is not automatic. Sobriety does not guarantee family growth, it will only potentiate it. Just as the family does not cause alcoholism, sobriety does not cause an immediately healthy family.

The initial stages of sobriety may contain some pitfalls. For example, the family probably has waited a long time for sobriety to occur and now that it has, they expect to enter "paradise." Many times in alcoholic families the longer the alcoholism continues the higher the probability that all family problems are blamed on the bottle. Therefore, with the cessation of drinking the family expects other problems to be eliminated. But difficulties will continue to exist, as they do in all families. Difficulties which were formerly believed to be related to alcoholism surface as ordinary, normal, family disagreements. In the past these problems may have been denied as was the alcoholism but now new ways of dealing with normal family problems will be needed.

However, some families have heard promises of sobriety before and will take a "wait and see" attitude before committing themselves to the family recovery process. Other families, however, will be more active and supportive of the new found sobriety and will be eager for many of the normal family behaviors that have been missing.

The Dry Drunk

For those families that are not able to join in the recovering process from alcoholism, much of their lives will remain the same. That is, even though sobriety has occurred, no other changes in the family are taking place because the results of the previous breakdown in family communications continue to take their toll on the emotions of family members. Unless the family is able to adapt to the sober alcoholic and themselves, and can establish and grow as a unit, the family may find itself on a "dry drunk." In such cases, tension, anxiety and conflict persist because other problems have not been solved. The family needs to understand that throughout the drinking period family relationships were deteriorating or were never sufficiently established. Some children in the "dry drunk" situation are unable to remember anything but drinking behavior on the part of one or both parents. The recovering alcoholic may, in fact, be trying to parent properly, but since this is a new or strange behavior, it may not be entirely trusted within the family when the drinking stops. The family must be incorporated in a new adaptive process. To ignore the role of the family in helping the recovering alcoholic support his or her sobriety, is to ignore the emotional impact that alcoholism has had on the family.

Family Growth

For those family members who can integrate the alcoholic back into the family and emotionally integrate themselves, their lives will get better. With this integration comes the potential for family growth. This family growth will mean that the family does not dwell on the past, nor hide the past, but has learned from it. The growing family is one that goes beyond the past. It continues to change and improve moving towards the goal of healthy family relationships. It is a family that is overcoming the negative influences of alcoholism and is united. As stated earlier, unfortunately, this does not happen often enough.

Family Interrelationships

What are the effects of all this adaptation and change? Many alcoholics are not aware of the emotional hazards they unthinkingly cause for their young. These effects, if considered at all, are seen as latent in the home, but may be seen as manifest by others outside the home. In order to consider the impact of these effects, some of the dynamics occurring in the home should be noted.

It is critical to consider whether or not both parents are alcoholic. In cases where both parents are involved in alcoholism, physical as well as emotional needs of the children may be unmet. When parents are unable or unwilling to assist in the home, their children may be consistently forced to organize and run the household. They may be picking up after parents and assuming extremely mature roles for their ages.

Time of onset of parental alcoholism is also an important consideration. Were the children born into an alcoholic home, or did parental addiction occur later in their life—and at what age? It is fairly well agreed upon in various educational studies that the impacts of emotional crises upon children are more detrimental at some ages than at others. Many children will experience an emotional separation from their parents, often feeling rejected by both parents even though only one is alcoholic. Lack of emotional security, and inability to discriminate between love as a noun and love as a verb, take their toll on many children of irresponsible parents. Alcoholic behavior in the family can prohibit intimate involvement and clearly impede the development of essential family bonds. When children's emotional needs have been stunted by neglect or destroyed by cruelty, the traditional image of parents as mentors and guides for their offspring becomes a farce. Clearly, the generally agreed upon signifiance of the positive influence of parents in the early education of children becomes questionable (Brookover and Erickson, 1975). It cannot be assumed that the proper parental roles toward education are being met, let alone attempted, in the alcoholic home.

The roles their parents play in the family are of critical important in the development of children. When a parent is alcoholic, parental roles are too often marked by inconsistency; and inconsistency is exhibited by both the alcoholic and the nonalcoholic parent. The alcoholic parent behaves like several different individuals with conflicting reactions and unpredictable attitudes. Often his or her role performance is dictated by successive periods of drunken behavior, remorse or guilt followed by high degrees of anxiety and tension, and finally, complete sobriety. Children may learn through experience to adapt themselves to such role inconsistency and even to develop some form of predictability; but little emotional security is found. What emotional security is available is usually obtainable only during periods of sobriety, and then only if other family issues are not producing tension.

A typical example of this kind of cycle goes as follows. On Friday night and all day Saturday the alcoholic is drunk. Sunday and Monday are hangover or recovery days, commonly marked by some degree of guilt or remorse. The middle of the week is the most normal. As the next weekend approaches, the alcoholic is being dominated by increasing anxiety and tension precipitating another drinking episode.

The children in such a situation learn that whatever is needed, physically or emotionally, must be obtained in the middle of the week. These become the "gettin" days when the getting may be more optimal because it is at this time, if any, that parenting or positive stroking by the alcoholic will occur. This is also the time that many unrealistic as well as realistic promises are made, which may or may not be kept. Normal promises made on good days may go unfulfilled because the collection day is one of inebriation. Sometimes this results in the making of still bigger and more elaborate promises, which are in turn broken. Occasions when promises are kept are sporadic, so cannot be relied on, again adding to the inconsistency. The alcoholic may show exaggerated concern or love one day and mistreat the child the next day. It is little wonder that a major problem for such children is a lack of trust and security in relationships with an alcoholic parent.

The nonalcoholic parent is hampered in attempting to fulfill the needs of the children because he or she is usually under constant tension over what is happening or may happen. Even when the alcoholic is sober, the spouse tends to suspect that the situation is tenuous, and consequently cannot support the alcoholic's attempts to win respect and approval—knowing that the probability of consistency is low. The nonalcoholic parent, who is subjected to and controlled by the inconsistent nature of the alcoholic, may become so engrossed in trying to fulfill two roles that he or she is unable to fulfill one role adequately with any type of consistency. Just as the alcoholic fluctuates between different levels of sobriety and emotionalism, so does the nonalcoholic parent react to these positions. As a result, the nonalcoholic parent may be just as guilty as the alcoholic in showing too much concern for the children at times and too little at other times. In addition, the spouse, worried about the effects of alcoholic behavior in the family situation, is apt to become too protective of or fearful for the children. This protection is often misunderstood by the children, especially when it is negatively administered in the form of warnings against certain places or people, without explanation.

Perhaps must of the nonalcoholic spouse's parental concern is justified by the fact that as many as forty to sixty percent of the children of alcoholic parents become alcoholics themselves (Hindman, 1975). Much has been written about the causal factors for this phenomenon. The question is centered around the nature-nurture controversy surrounding alcoholism. Is alcoholism genetically based or are other factors present? This author believes that the nurturing aspects play the more prominent role and that the damage inflicted on the child is not limited to preadolescence or adolescence, but has long-range implications.

Although not directly related to drinking practices, additional evidence that the nurture impact is the stronger influence is shown by the fact that children of alcoholic parents are more affected by the disharmony and rejection in the home life than by the drinking. They see that drinking stops once in a while, though the fighting and tension continue. This constant state of agitation affects personality development. More particularly, children observe the use of alcohol as a method of dealing with uncomfortable situations. Although the children may vow not to drink and are cognizant of the potential harm of alcohol abuse, this position may give way to use of drinking as a means of escape during real or perceived crises in later life.

The two-parent family in which alcoholism affects one or both partners cannot provide a healthy parental relationship. A single, nonalcoholic parent can give children a healthier atmosphere. In a family where one of the parents is alcoholic, the other parent will not be able to singly overcome all of the impacts of the other's drinking; he or she cannot provide a separate environment because both parental roles are distorted or inconsistent. The nonalcoholic parent devotes energy in trying to deal with the alcoholic at various phases of adaptation, leaving little energy for the needs of the offspring. Often the children are forced into a position of increased responsibilities and unfamiliar roles. The eldest child may be put in charge of smaller children or be drawn into the role of confidant for the nonalcoholic spouse.

Sometimes children find themselves abandoned in the middle or forced to choose sides, either of which can lead to withdrawal and a preference to be left alone. It was earlier mentioned that family disengagement from contact with others is a form of adapting behavior to the alcoholic problem. Disengagement can also occur within the family itself. The children avoid family contact as often as possible, having learned that minimal contact may also mean minimal discomfort. Such children want only to be left alone. They no longer feel close to either parent. The need to be isolated from their parents' conflicts may carry over to their attitudes toward other adults. Such children associate solitude with absence of conflict; thus, being alone is not always as feared as we might expect; it may be viewed as a pleasant time of relaxation.

Affection or emotional support outside the home is a vital aspect in helping such children. It will be considered in subsequent chapters.

Many families can become recovered, or recovering, families. Many will not without assistance from others. Outside support becomes critical to this process, especially when we remember that there may be no support from within the family. Often children need help in acquiring or regaining a sense of trust in their parents and others.

Also vital to the children is the acquisition of self-awareness and self-esteem. Basic to a family recovery program is the question of whether the children can grow up to face life successfully. Will they be able to achieve a sense of security, to be able to grow while accepting their circumstances, and more importantly, to feel good about themselves?

When working with the children of alcoholic parents, alcoholism (and not just the alcoholic) should be addressed. The entire picture can be brought into focus and invisible symptoms, as well as easily-observed ones, can be discussed.

2

The Children: Their World and Their Perceptions

Not all children of alcoholic parents suffer identical emotional effects; in fact, some seem to survive quite well. Accounting for this are a variety of factors, such as age of onset of parental alcoholism, number of children in the family, ordinal position, friends outside of the family, and which parent is the alcoholic. However, it appears that of the studies involving these children, we can generalize into two broad categories, the "haves" and the "have nots." *What they have or do not have is an ability within themselves to establish positive primary relationships outside the home.*

The importance of the primary relationship for the development of a child is well established. It appears that although most primary relationships occur within the home, for many children of alcoholic parents these relationships are developed outside the home and are able to achieve virtually the same importance in the life of the child. Perhaps for the child of alcoholic parents it is not so important that primary relationships are established in the home, but that they are established somewhere. The issue of primary relationships becomes a determining factor. It will be further elaborated when addressing the role of the school and its personnel.

Although not all children of alcoholic parents are affected in the same way, there are some experiences (and, more particularly, reactions to these experiences) that all these children endure and share, regardless of the outcome of the experience. Many studies show that children in the "have not" category exhibit such problems as delinquency, anxiety, and depression. In addition, much research indicates that these youngsters may have poor self-concepts, are easily frustrated, perform poorly in school (probably due to the former characteristics), and are more likely to suffer adjustment problems (Chafetz, 1971; Jackson, 1954; McKay, 1963; Nylander, 1958; Fine, 1975). What then do the children see and how do they feel about their situations that may contribute to such findings?

THE YOUNG WORLD

"We all just go off and nurse our wounds . . . nobody cares how you feel" (Cork, 1969). This statement made by a child of alcoholic parents, stated to Margaret Cork, reveals much insight into the unseen world of these children. The children possess opinions—often very clear opinions—about their situations and the behavior of their parents.

When such children discuss their parents to counselors, parental role inconsistency is a major theme. The same is true when parents are discussing their children. The only difference may be that the alcoholic is putting forth inconsistency and the children are forced to accept it, thus reacting to it in behavioral patterns that normal situations would not make necessary. The parents are actors and the children become reactors. Because they receive inconsistency, they are forced to react to it in ways that are consistent neither with their roles as children nor with their basic personalities.

Often children of alcoholics see themselves as extremely mature for their age. This is due to the fact that they are often called upon to act more grown-up than their parents. They must anticipate their reactions to the parents' actions and, therefore, limit and subjugate many childhood mannerisms. They consciously choose to curb their feelings and behavior in order "not to rock the boat." This behavior can be described as "hypermaturity"—the young person is engaging in behavior that would not be expected of one of his or her chronological age. However, any negative consequences of hypermaturity may not be readily noticeable to adults. The hypermature child is usually very responsible, can handle leadership positions, takes charge of situations and outwardly displays competent behavior. This type of behavior is valued by adults and therefore is seldom seen as having negative developmental consequences for the child. However, inwardly for the children this form of accelerated development can cause high degrees of role inconsistency where the child is physically a young adolescent, but feels the responsibilities of an adult.

In essence, these children constantly monitor their own behavior, frequently at the expense of creating feelings of conflict, resentment, anxiety, and anger within themselves. Another reaction to these demands — one which causes great stress for the children — is that of their own ambivalence. They may find themselves loving the person who drinks, but hating the drinking.

Children see parental behavior as a reflection of their own worth. Children of alcoholics tend to feel that because there is something wrong in their family, there is something wrong with them. In time, they begin to realize that their home and their family are different from those of their friends. In their homes, (unlike in normal ones), family relationships and functions are regulated by the condition of the alcoholic. It becomes difficult for children to return to their own homes after being in their friends' homes, experiencing "normal" family relationships. This difficulty is further compounded by the fact that the family, as described in Chapter One, may be attempting to deny, cover up, or eliminate the problem without revealing it to outside sources. Too often the thoughts and emotions of such children remain unshared with friends, because on the one hand they may be under orders from their nonalcoholic parent to say nothing or to pretend; on the other hand they may feel embarrassed and fearful that friends cannot understand their predicament. Worse yet, they may fear ridicule or rejection from friends. Even within the home, siblings may isolate themselves, instead of sharing feelings of mutual endurance. Much of children's modeling behavior is taken from their parents, and it should be of no surprise that the children of alcoholic parents often argue more than others, thus finding little psychological comfort from other brothers and sisters.

Sibling relationships are further complicated by the roles that may be placed upon individual brothers and sisters. In many cases the oldest child may be called upon to take a great deal of responsibility for the other children, which not only places role strain on the child, but also puts him or her in competition with the parent whose job the child is attempting to fill. The oldest may soon tire of the unwanted position and resent the feelings of the displaced parent as well as the feelings of his or her siblings.

Another uncomfortable situation occurs when the eldest becomes the constant source of ventilation and support for the nonalcoholic parent.

Outside the home, oldest children may experience role inconsistency when coming under the influence of other adults. In school, for example, they must revert back to their original role of adolescent, student, sophomore, etc., where a few hours before and a few hours in the future they will again be faced with the responsibility of helping to raise the family of an alcoholic.

An additional example of role inconsistency is shown in the work of Sharon Wegscheider (1979) who offers four different primary roles often occupied by children of alcoholics. These are the childhood roles of being the *family hero, scapegoat, lost child* or *mascot.* The family hero is usually the oldest child and displays behaviors that are extremely mature for him or her and is considered highly competent. The scapegoat traditionally is the target of family frustrations and confusion. Often these feelings are internalized by the scapegoat, but may be outwardly displayed by negative behavior. The lost children, usually the middle children, are probably those children suffering the most role inconsistency. Unlike the other siblings' roles which are specifically defined, the lost child's identity is uncertain. They are literally lost regarding where they fit in the family. The role of mascot is often identified with the youngest child. This child may be overly protected from the family problems resulting in the child becoming overly dependent.

In addition to the above roles, there may be another category of children from troubled families. These children have been called *"invulnerables"* (Garmezy, 1976). These are the children, that despite all the family problems, have not only survived, but also have grown into healthy adults. It has been estimated that approximately ten percent of children in troubled homes have been invulnerables.

In summary, for children of alcoholics, roles range from being rigidly defined to total ambiguity. Obviously, such role inconsistency only adds to an already unstable situation.

THE YOUNG OPINION

According to limited studies in this field, children of alcoholic parents have certain specific attitudes in common about alcoholism in the family.

One finding is that an alcoholic mother is regarded by children as more detrimental than an alcoholic father. Societal disapproval may play a large role here, as well as the obvious role of mother-child bonding and relationship. Research also indicates that in cases where the mother is alcoholic, there are more behavioral and emotional problems for the children (Cork, 1969). Female alcoholics usually suffer more societal disdain and reaction than do male alcoholics. Also, the male traditionally has fewer hours of contact with the children, particularly when they are young.

Traditional roles could also affect how alcoholism is handled in the family. If the alcoholic is male, the tolerance level and at times even acceptability for his behavior will be relatively higher, and it will be endured for a longer period of time, than if the alcoholic is female.

Patterns of time that elapse during the process of becoming alcoholic vary according to sex. Currently in our society, the durations of time between social drinking, problem drinking, and alcoholism are shorter for women than for men. This phenomenon is not totally explainable, but certainly the societal reactions to the woman's drinking increases the amount of stress, anxiety, and perhaps guilt that the woman may be enduring.

Another fact revealed by studies is that children consider fighting in the home worse than the drinking it accompanies. The children can find some respite from the drinking, but not from the fighting and constant tension caused by alcoholism. One of the hardest problems for children is not the acceptance of parental drinking, but trying to understand the relationship between their parents. Unable to understand that it is a drug-affected relationship, they have difficulty understanding why their parents constantly argue or why they have little emotional involvement with each other. They are puzzled as to why the couple stays together; on the other hand, when separation occurs, what little security they have is shattered. The children's feelings are reflected in loss of sleep, feelings of hopelessness, and alienation from the family and from themselves; they feel totally powerless to make the situation disappear. They come to consider themselves pawns in a game which they do not understand, or victims of a battle they cannot escape.

Because of lack of family closeness, the children are deprived of normal family fun. There are few enjoyable activities because family life is structured around the alcohol problem, or avoided because of it, or ends up being influenced by it. Consequently, "have" children who are able to carry over primary relationships tend to seek outside activities and possible close contacts outside the immediate family. However, if a child is in the "have not" category, in which all primary relationships are stunted or absent, any outside relationships he or she forms will tend to be characterized by insecurity, fear, and a lack of trust in others. By holding back the giving and receiving of affection, "have nots" literally reject the thing that they desire. This holding back restricts the opportunities for outside fun, which makes it evident why many studies indicate that children of alcoholic parents have little involvement in community activities. Feelings of detachment and lack of trust in others leave such children with little peer support.

Another effect on attitudes of children of alcoholics derives from emotional abuse in the home. The youngsters are expected to endure many storms, with few opportunities for ventilation of their own feelings. The domination of parental alcoholism deprives them of the opportunity to cope with their own emotions.

Unfortunately, help is rarely accessible to these children. Because of limited programs and even more limited information on access to them, the children rarely seek help themselves. If any help is received, it usually comes as an indirect result of some other family problem or of a child's own behavioral problems at school or elsewhere outside the home. Even then, such attention seldom discovers the actual family situation.

Alcoholics may move beyond emotional abuse to physical abuse as their involvement with drinking increases. The relationship between child abuse and alcoholism is an old one. Spouse beating also causes much suffering to children who must witness it, or who become drawn into the violence when coming to the aid of an abused parent.

(See Appendix for resources on Child Abuse)

The instinct to survive is strong in everyone. Children who feel abandoned, torn by conflict between parents, or helpless to cope with an alcoholic parent will attempt various methods of saving themselves. "Have not" children are apt to choose disassociation from the family and avoidance of close contacts with others. The "have" child is better able to form outside ties and to assume adult responsibilities, and this often brings admiration from neighbors, teachers, and peers who may not understand it as the by-product of a stressful situation. "Have" children may be extremely mature for their age; and since they are forced to do much for themselves and perhaps other family members, this ability spills over into other situations. However, these children are not seen as acting out their problems because "acting out" is usually considered as a negative behavior. In reality they may be acting out, but their actions are part of the "unseen casualty" syndrome. Children who overcompensate by growing up too soon bear their own kinds of scars inflicted by alcoholism in the home.

Studies indicate that parental drinking is most detrimental for children of six to seven, in early adolescence, and again in later adolescence (Bosma, 1975). Family disengagement is accomplished by those children in all three age brackets who are able to discover mechanisms to achieve it. Children in late adolescence often see their solution as physical disengagement, and move out of the home environment if they possibly can. It is highly probable that many cases of educational dropout can be attributed to parental alcoholism.

This chapter began with the statement that the children of alcoholic parents feel no one cares, and this feeling is frequently carried over into school activities and social life outside the home. Parents who are absorbed in problems brought on by alcoholism do not attend to their youngster's school activities or other involvements. The children may feel that there are no parental expectations concerning how they do in school because as long as they are doing "OK"—which may be minimal—their activities are unnoticed.

3

Human Development and Personality Among Children of Alcoholics

Environment has a profound influence on physical, emotional, and personality development of children; in fact, it is generally considered to be the dominating factor in human development.

Development is seen to reflect either biological or environmental influences which result in changes in the structure, thought, or behavior of a person (Craig, 1976). Biological development involves processes of physical growth, aging, and maturation, while environmental development involves circumstances surrounding an individual, with which he or she interacts emotionally and socially to form an individual personality structure. Obviously, human development is a blend of these two influences and their interreactions.

Many schools of thought, Piaget, Freud, Skinner, Maslow, Mead, and Sullivan, all analyze the human development of children. Constant to these various models is the analysis of human development from the perspective of a "normal" or ideal type with normal growth patterns or stages serving as models.

In the case of children of alcoholics, however, levels of development may not always be normal. Children of alcoholics are apt to encounter developmental aspects with environmental implications different from those met by the child of nonalcoholic parents. Some of these differences will have detrimental effects; others will not. In individual cases it is not possible to predict which will or will not, since each child's development is unique and dependent upon a building-block theory of internalizing experiences. Not all experiences are equally recorded by different children. This chapter will attempt to raise some of the developmental concerns for children of alcoholics regarding physical, emotional, and personality considerations.

PHYSICAL DEVELOPMENT

Developmental concerns for children of alcoholic parents begin at the prenatal stage. Whether the child is born of an alcoholic mother or lives with an alcoholic father, detrimental aspects are present in the environment.

In the case of an alcoholic mother, the "fetal alcohol syndrome" can develop (Jones, Smith, Ulleland, Streissgoth, 1973). This syndrome results in the physical underdevelopment of the fetus and according to research, the retardation of growth is not reversible. Also attributable to this syndrome are subnormal intelligence and lagging motor development. The syndrome results from poor physical condition of the alcoholic mother, plus the fact that alcohol ingested by the mother enters the blood system of the fetus. Children of alcoholic mothers often bear their children prematurely. These children are usually of low birth weight and suffer from a high rate of infant mortality. A problem foremost in alcoholics is vitamin deficiency. In the case of alcoholic mothers, this problem is compounded due to the vital role of vitamins in nourishment of the fetus.

The use of any drugs, particularly during the first three months of pregnancy, is dangerous. Most drug users are multiple drug users; they not only take the drug of their choice, but may also smoke and use other drugs to relieve all sorts of physical discomfort. The alcohol syndrome coupled with the use of other drugs can damage the fetus and also reduce the chances for later normal physical development of the child.

Physical development of the fetus can also be impaired when the father is the alcoholic partner. Effects of

anxiety and stress on expectant mothers have been established by research. Constant worrying about present conditions and fear of future problems after the baby arrives can
drain heavily upon the psychological resources of a preg-
nant woman.

At this point in time, it is not known to what extent
alcoholism affects heredity or whether or not there is an
inherited tendency to become alcoholic. Although various
perspectives have been offered, no conclusive evidence has
been presented on either side.

Physical concerns are important throughout a child's
life. Later in this chapter, during discussions of stages of
development, the physical aspect will be more closely
examined. However, one physical consideration that can
occur at any time in the environment of a child is physical
child abuse. The relationship between alcoholism and child
abuse is high, as children often become victims of the conflict experienced by their parents. It is important to realize
that not only may the alcoholic be a child abuser, but the
nonalcoholic may be one as well. Thus, the effects of stress
and forms of physical abuse can cause mental, physical,
and emotional damage to the victims (Solomon, 1973).
The consequences of being physically beaten or attacked,
as well as the fear of these behaviors, have implications for
development far beyond the physical harm suffered. Probably the most disturbing aspect of this situation is that

approximately one-half of the abused children who are returned by the courts to their parents eventually die of
further abuse or neglect (Fontana, 1976).

EMOTIONAL ASPECTS

It goes without saying that emotional development is
a prime factor in personality development; how a child
develops emotionally will influence how the child sees and
can handle the world. Regardless of how many normal
emotions may be experienced during development, children of alcoholics will also experience the emotions of fear
and anxiety at various times. These feelings are present in
all people, but for these children normal emotional development may not be sufficient to overcome them.

Central to skill in handling negative emotions is presence of a sense of security in relationships with other
people. For children, security is usually found in the family, but in alcoholic families it is not always present. Absence of security can often produce undesirable or destructive defense mechanisms in children of alcoholics.

Throughout their development children are consistently confronted with change. They must face the challenge of growth, plus the necessity to maintain the security

of the past. Children of alcoholics encouter enormous growth problems, but possess little security from the past upon which to draw. In light of this, much of their childhood and perhaps their adult emotional development will be characterized by powerful defense mechanisms. Among these are regression, repression, sublimation, projection, and reaction formations (Papalia and Olds, 1978).

Regression

In times of an alcohol crisis, children may regress to an earlier level of emotional or behavioral development by attempting to go back to a previous state of security (assuming that one existed). When the crisis has passed, they will return to their normal level of emotional development. This type of defense mechanism can be extremely complicated if the child has no solid sense of previous security on which to draw. Continued repetition of alcoholic crises serves to compound the complications.

Repression

Repression is closely associated with anxiety-producing situations. It results in children negating feelings that are normally freely expressed. Children of alcoholics frequently repress their feelings in order to prevent "rocking the boat." They may also repress actions; for example, when deciding not to invite friends to their home because of the fear of unintended consequences.

Sublimation

Sublimation involves directing feelings of discomfort or anxiety to acceptable activities. Attempts at sublimation by children of alcoholics tend to be seen as positive aspects by most adults. A child's becoming a "workaholic" in school could be based upon sublimation of undesirable home conditions.

Projection

Projection means denial of unacceptable behaviors or situations by attributing them to others. Thus a child in an alcoholic home might ignore his or her own inappropriate behavior while (unrealistically) blaming another for the same behavior. The mechanism here functions to allow the child to disassociate from realities he or she cannot bear to face.

Reaction Formation

Reaction formation is characterized by expression of the opposite of one's true feelings. The adolescent whose situation is known by his or her peers may consistently make jokes and light-hearted remarks about his or her home situation, when in reality the child is totally frustrated.

These above methods of coping with stress are all found in the emotional development of most children of alcoholics. Aside from the normal emotions associated with "growing" pains, children of alcoholics must handle a variety of emotions for which they may be ill-equipped due to an inadequate state of emotional development.

As emotional development continues, the child takes on a sense of identity or self-concept. Much of this self-concept is derived from the child's measuring his adequacy as defined by others (Oswald, 1976). With the constant use of defense mechanisms, a true self-concept may never emerge. Some children of alcoholics feel that they were and are unwanted. They see themselves in positions of inferiority, inadequacy, and even worthlessness. Although such children behave in ways to generate the opinions others have of them, feedback they get from others serves to confirm their negative self-concepts.

PERSONALITY

Regardless of what theory is used to examine personality, all theories concur that much of one's personality is made up of life experiences. Many theorists of human development and personality divide life experiences into stages, each stage typified by different conflicts and crises which must be overcome in order to achieve adequate levels of development. It has also been postulated that each successive stage functions as building blocks for future stages. For many children of alcoholics the crises confronted in successive stages are compounded by unsolved problems left over from previous stages, plus the continuing stresses caused by living with an alcoholic parent. This compounding effect can have detrimental consequences for adequate personality development.

To illustrate these stages of compounded problems, the life stages of Erik Erikson are used under the next heading (Erikson, 1963). Erikson's concepts were chosen because they are based more upon society's effect on a person rather than the person's effect on society. Children of alcoholics are often overwhelmed by their environment and have little chance to act upon it. At each stage of development Erikson sees particular conflicts that must be resolved in a positive manner. The success or failure of this resolution affect the handling of conflicts at future stages. As time passes, the child begins to establish a collection of positive and/or negative outcomes. If outcomes are mostly positive, the child will be better able to handle later adult roles.

(As mentioned earlier, not all children of alcoholic parents are affected in the same manner. Some will emerge from stages in their lives with a high ratio of positive conflict or crisis resolutions. Others will not.)

ALCOHOLISM
AND THE STAGES OF DEVELOPMENT

Trust Versus Mistrust

Erikson sees a sense of trust as the most vital element of a healthy personality. The formation of trust begins at birth and is crucial during the first year of life, when the infant is completely dependent on the fulfillment of basic needs. Maternal deprivation by an alcoholic mother can undermine the establishment of an infant's trust. The needs of the child may be ignored, attended as a last resort, or begrudgingly administered.

Even in cases where a baby's physical needs are satisfied, trust may not be established because of lack of emotional stability. The quantity of interactions of the relationship may not be as important as the quality. Whether the mother or father is alcoholic, the emotional drain on the parents may be so great that there is little emotional support left on which the child may rely. The seriousness of alcoholic parental role-inconsistency is gravely under-estimated at this level because the child is nonverbal and helpless. Erikson feels that without a basic sense of trust in infancy the crises of later stages will be difficult to handle.

Not all children of alcoholics are born into alcoholic homes. Parental alcoholism may occur at later stages in their development. Those children who have established a sense of trust may be better able to handle the onset of alcoholism in a parent.

Autonomy Versus Shame and Doubt

A child must be able to achieve autonomy and yet accept the useful guidance of others. The contribution of parents during a child's growth is to administer reasonable and firm guidance when the quest for autonomy goes too far; a delicate balance between cooperation and willfulness is needed. In cases of excessive restrictions, autonomy is not achieved and is overshadowed by an emerging sense of shame in the child. A parent who wants to protect his or her child from the home environment may unwittingly limit childhood growth. The child is denied the opportunity to develop a sense of self-control because all forms of control, usually administered through restrictions, are supplied. The child may not be able to develop sufficient autonomy, resulting in a self-concept of inadequacy and shame.

Initiative Versus Guilt

Conflicts between initiative and guilt feelings begin in a four or five-year-old child, when his or her curiosity about the world is treated as inappropriate by adults. The child's questions are hushed up or ignored; sometimes even games and normal playful activities are stopped short or prohibited by parental commands that cause feelings of guilt in the child. In alcoholic homes such restrictions may be prevalent in the parent-child relationship because all family behavior is being dictated by the self-centeredness of the alcoholic.

Thus a balance between parental restrictiveness and permissiveness becomes desirable as the child grows; and consistency is the most important ingredient in this balance.

Erikson feels that inconsistency does more harm than being slightly too restrictive. Guilt emerges in the child when the responses to his or her behavior are unpredictable. In alcoholic homes inconsistency is a dominating factor. To overcome this the child may choose to over-conform, at the expense of subjugating initiative and creativity.

This stage is also characterized by observation and imitating of adult behavior. Role modeling, when performed by an alcoholic, can give a child inappropriate concepts of adult roles. The child sees alcoholism as an integral part of the role being played by either or both parents. It may not be until later years that some children realize that what they had observed was not normal adult behavior.

Industry Versus Inferiority

The typical child entering elementary school begins to develop a need to feel useful, commensurate with his or her growing ability to explore and achieve. This is what Erikson calls a "sense of industry." A crisis at this stage occurs if a sense of inadequacy or inferiority becomes dominant over the sense of industry. Although problems at this period are mostly concerned with school environment, a lack of parental interest in the child's accomplishments can compound the child's sense of inferiority, since the influence of parents on education during the elementary school years is particularly strong.

In the alcoholic home, feelings of uselessness can emerge in a child which will carry over into the school situation. A child who attempts varying behaviors or initiates actions that he or she hopes will be useful in alleviating problems at home, only to meet with failure at home, will tend to approach school feeling useless.

The elementary school child needs to feel that he or she is achieving goals, both educationally and socially; parents of the elementary school child possess the key to providing him or her with a sense of accomplishment. Survival in school—the child's first step outside his or her primary environment—can depend upon the amount of self-esteem the child has developed within the home, plus the amount of support provided by parents when the child encounters school problems. Parents who show little interest in the child's school life may question poor performance in the upper grades and never realize their own contribution to the child's lack of success. Alcoholic parents may value education very highly, but because of drinking, guilt, and stress, they may be unable to provide the behavior necessary to help their child succeed in school.

Learning Identity Versus Identity Diffusion

The question "Who am I?" is closely related to development during adolescence. The crisis of this period evolves from normal attempts to establish a clear sense of identity. The adolescent is no longer identified as a child, but is not considered an adult.

Overidentification with negative characteristics is a problem that can occur at this stage. The adolescent sees himself or herself in terms of negative attitudes and rebellious actions. In alcoholic families such feelings are often already present, because the entire family feels deviant, making it more than normally difficult for the teenager to search for individual identity. A sense of personal identity is overshadowed by family identity.

If this identity stage has been entered with a previously-developed sense of inferiority, the crisis is intensified. Children who have been told that they are failures, inadequate, or have feelings of being unwanted are thus set up for later self-fulfilling prophecies.

Intimacy Versus Isolation

This stage is concerned with the ability to establish intimate relations with others. As previously mentioned, the ability to establish primary relations with others may be the single most important consideration for children of alcoholics.

When close relationships are unattainable, feelings of isolation arise. The young adult is hindered at a time when most people are sharing feelings and developing satisfying communication with others. An adolescent from an alcoholic home who is unable to achieve intimacy "has so much to live with and so little to live for" (Oswald, 1976). Such young adults may repress all inner feelings while displaying an outer pretense at being "normal." Such repression can result in loss of ability to become "card-carrying members of the human race."

Children who emerge emotionally affected from an alcoholic home may find themselves socially isolated. They have not had the opportunity to develop the life skills necessary to become fully functioning adults. They are forced to remain within themselves. The next stage of development is even more difficult.

Generativity Versus Self-Absorption

The effects of parental alcoholism do not disappear when offspring leave the home. Once patterns have been established they may continue throughout adulthood. Erikson assumes that the normal mature adult is capable of intimacy and possesses a strong identity. He feels that, in addition to these, the adult should have positive qualities to pass on to future generations. Some adults become parents, however, and have little to offer their children that could be called positive. They have been deprived of learning how to form interactions with others, so are paralyzed in relationships with their children. Unless such parents are able to overcome these problems, it is highly probable that the effects of being raised in an alcoholic family are passed along to at least one more generation. This becomes particularly frightening if children of alcoholics become alcoholic themselves and the process is continued.

Surviving an alcoholic home may take all a child has, so that in later life there is nothing left to give. The new adult is faced with psychological impoverishment. This becomes particularly frustrating to those who counted the days until they could leave the home environment, only to find that they do not possess the ability to improve their lives.

Integrity Versus Disgust

Erikson's last stage is development of integrity in the adult. A sense of integrity involves acceptance of responsibility for one's own life without blaming others for past or present misfortune. Unless children of alcoholics are able to achieve success at the previous life stages, this last stage appears to be impossible to attain.

When integrity is not developed, the individual finds it hard to accept life as it is. The person remains immaturely dependent on outside circumstances and makes statements such as, "I never could do what I want," or "If I had it to do over again, it would all be different."

ENVIRONMENTAL FEEDBACK

A final consideration for children who grow up in alcoholic homes is that they are influenced by their parents and consequently may develop similar personality characteristics. Although it is commonly agreed that there is no "alcoholic personality," it has been established that many alcoholics share certain personality characteristics such as anxiety, dependency, immaturity, inferiority, depression, and low self-esteem (Forrest, 1975). If such characteristics are learned from role modeling, one can easily see that problems borne by children of alcoholics may be compounded when they reach adulthood. Many children of alcoholic parents become alcoholic themselves and the cyclical process continues to gain victims. This process seems assured, unless substitute environmental situations can attempt to counteract the disorganization and uncertainty of the home and family life. The potential source of positive actions to which we now turn is the school.

Winter

Here coms dad in a car
he is going to a bar
and the bar is very
far
but It is snowing out
side
but he's going for
a ride
He's going for a ride
but I thought he was
going to the bar
He is going to the
bar for some beer.

This poem was written by Kevin, a third grader.

PART B

SUGGESTIONS FOR EDUCATORS

4

The Role of the School and the Teacher

Any school's program for children of alcoholic parents should be aimed specifically at the children themselves. The school should not become involved in the rehabilitation of alcoholic parents. On the surface, it may appear that working with the alcoholic parent is necessary. However, intervention involving treatment of parental alcoholism is outside the school's sphere of authority and probable competency.

Working with the children of alcoholics may appear to be an indirect approach; in some aspects this is true. But the school is not in the rehabilitation business. The school is in the education business, and direct involvement here means working directly with and in helping students. If through the school's efforts a change should occur in an alcoholic parent, this should be considered an incidental (albeit beneficial) side-effect.

AREAS OF SCHOOL CONCERN

A successful school program for children of alcoholic parents should be able to provide help by:

- Helping students to learn about alcohol and alcoholism.

- Helping teachers to deal with their own feelings toward alcohol use.

- Helping teachers to be perceived by their students as credible regarding alcohol use.

- Setting the right objectives for alcohol education.

- Developing a valid content for alcohol education.

- Involving students as active participants in alcohol education rather than as mere recipients of information.

- Helping children of alcoholics to express themselves—which many have difficulty doing.

- Helping children of alcoholics to gain an appropriate identity.

- Helping students to effectively relate to alcoholics and nonalcoholics.

- Referring children of alcoholics to other services when they can benefit from such assistance.

- Identifying children of alcoholic parents as part of an individualized educational program.

TEACHING ABOUT ALCOHOL

Aside from experiencing alcoholism's behavioral consquences, most children do not understand alcoholism or know what it is. Children from alcoholic homes tend to consider their circumstances unique and isolated. Education regarding the true facts about alcoholism clarifies the facts for such children. Myths must be exposed and disproved. Through various types of special classes, or by incorporating the subject into various existing classes, the school can provide information about alcohol and alcoholism (see *Appendices* for suggested sources). A primary purpose of educational efforts in this area is to provide some relief through knowledge. Whether or not the home situation is solved, asking questions and obtaining true facts can provide some relief.

Since it is not possible to identify the children of alcoholics in all cases, comprehensive alcohol education should be provided in the classroom, where it should be treated as factually as any other subject. Under no circumstances should it be limited to education about living with an alcoholic parent. A realistic overview of the problem, presented from a neutral position, can supply a frame of reference which enables students to make responsible choices. The theme of responsible drinking, for those who will choose to drink, offers the framework to assess the use of alcohol in American society in a realistic manner. It is obvious that the majority of people in our society are not anti-alcohol, but are opposed to alcohol abuse and abusive behavior.

Educational classes can serve as vehicles to identify children of alcoholic parents since many of these children may, during or after class, ask questions that will indicate to the teacher an existing or potential problem at home. Using the theme of responsible drinking may help to reduce the high percentage of the children of alcoholics who become alcoholic themselves, and whose parental role models have consistently demonstrated irresponsible drinking.

Children who are shy or reluctant to ask questions will be best served if a good supply of free pamphlets are provided in a highly accessible area. There are many organizations that provide pamphlets on alcohol and alcoholism with topics ranging from drinking and driving to advise for children of alcoholics (see *Appendices*). These pamphlets can usually be obtained free or at minimal cost. In many school libraries, books on alcoholism are often "missing" from the shelves. This indicates interest in the subject, but also indicates perceived embarrassment in checking the books out.

The Feelings of Teachers

In the early 1900's when alcohol education began to gain in popularity in America, the major theme in school was one of temperance in using alcohol. By the 1920's, however, this orientation of temperance shifted to reflect the prohibition movement. Abstinence was advocated. The effects of these themes in alcohol education of abstinence and temperance are difficult to evaluate. Certainly temperance or abstinence of alcohol use is not in itself harmful. However, the manner in which abstinence and temperance were pressed upon students may have produced a number of undesired results including beliefs about alcohol. Both the temperance and abstinence programs in schools through the 1920's contended that any amount of alcohol use was wrong and ·concentrated on the "disasterous" effects of drinking.

During the 1930's little was said about alcohol education. Perhaps this was in reaction to the repeal of prohibition. However, in the 1940's, the very negative aspects of alcohol use by adults (alcoholism, broken homes, and skid-row stories) were being emphasized in school programs. In the 1950's American schools broadened this concern to include teenage alcohol use while still stressing horror stories in teaching about alcohol. The evils of using alcohol became central material for courses.

During the 1960's alcohol education took a backseat to an emerging concern to stop the use among students of other drugs such as marijuana and amphetamines. The approach of drug education in the 1960's clearly followed the traditional mode. However, like the alcohol education programs, it was characterized by the scare tactics preceding it. The use of alcohol and other drugs by our youth was not impeded. In fact, during the early 1970's the use of alcohol by teenagers was almost applauded since it was considered a move away from the "drug scene." By the mid-seventies we were confronted with increasing reports of teenage alcoholism, and again approaches emphasizing the evils of drinking were stressed. In summary, alcohol education has remained in many schools what it was in the early 1900's.

One unfortunate result of seventy years of alcohol education tradition is that it has left present day educators with a "poor track record" in alcohol education and few guidelines for improvement. Teachers with responsibilities for alcohol education still face critical problems, and in facing them many are ill-prepared. Many lack confidence because they do not understand, in an objective way, the functions of alcohol.

Initially, teachers must examine their own attitudes about alcohol and their own drinking habits. If negativism is to be overcome in alcohol education, it must be replaced by objectivity. Our biases for or against alcohol will make this difficult. Many of our biased attitudes stem from personal drinking habits or our contact with those who drink. This contact can be responsible for biased positive or negative attitudes. One who has had unfortunate experiences because of the alcohol use of others and has not worked them out can be just as detrimental to desired educational endeavors as one whose own drinking habits are questionable. We cannot be so naive to assume that educators are immune to alcohol problems.

TEACHER CREDIBILITY

The subject of teacher credibility, regardless of subject taught, is an important consideration in effective teaching. Nowhere, however, has credibility in the classroom been challenged more than by those receiving alcohol and other drug education. Teacher credibility in these areas has suffered because of the lack of objectivity and a failure to be concerned with previous attempts to educate students regarding substance abuse. Much of credibility has to do with the relationship between the message given and the message received. Will students perceive the teacher as knowledgeable on these subjects? How will teachers handle the questions of "Do you drink?" or "Have you ever had too much to drink?" "What is too much?"

Credibility in alcohol education can be lost because of perceived personal bias in presentation. If one of the goals of alcohol education is to help students make their own choices, we should not be viewed as dictating preferences for them. Even if appropriate preferences are advocated, they may be seen as not realistic if the teacher is viewed as one who does not understand "today's world."

The issues of teacher credibility in alcohol education are similar to teacher credibility problems in other areas. The establishment of credibility is dependent upon many factors ranging from influence and power to knowledge and attractiveness. However, factual data presented in an objective manner which encourages honest responses from students will greatly enhance the teacher's credibility in alcohol education.

OBJECTIVES FOR ALCOHOL EDUCATION

As a prelude to gaining credibility, it will be helpful if the teachers of alcohol education become clear about what alcohol education includes and does not include, including objectives, content, and procedures. What is alcohol education? Does it consist of the effects of alcohol in the body, problems of alcoholism, how to live with an alcoholic, or guidelines on drinking and driving?

A severe problem of past alcohol education has been the almost universal lack of a clear definition of alcohol education. At the classroom level there is a need to decide upon what is alcohol education. Too often to fulfill a state requirement, a teacher is called upon to teach an alcohol education class or unit. "What do I teach?" is asked. "Oh, whatever you like; we need to complete ten hours of instruction" is mumbled in reply. What is needed is a clear statement of intent or teaching objectives that are attainable within the time frame of the course.

THE CONTENT OF ALCOHOL EDUCATION

Closely associated with the past lack in specifying the teaching objectives of alcohol education is the inconsistency of much of the course contents of a typical program.

For example, another problem concerns the appropriateness of the material for the given students. Alcohol education in the fifth grade should not be the same as in the senior year of high school. The needs of the students are different. In elementary school, although research indicates that the majority of students have already tried alcohol, their interests lie in what alcohol is and why people drink it. Students in the middle school years want to know specific details about alcohol, such as the different types of drinks, what happens to the body after using alcohol, how much is safe, and again why use alcohol. Senior high students' concerns are more directly related to the use of alcohol and behavioral consequences. Interest ranges from drinking and driving to health and personal problems associated with consumption. Another topic often discussed is the relationship to or comparison of alcohol with other drugs. Can one mix alcohol with other drugs? In other words, as students get older, their experiences with alcohol and their needs for information become more personal.

A course in alcohol education should be structured similar to the way other school subjects are taught throughout the educational process, i.e., history, science, etc. Most courses are taught on a building block assumption according to perceived levels of understanding and the difficulty of the material. The extensiveness of American history courses in elementary school are different from those of high school, yet it is the same topic. Alcohol education should be handled in a similar fashion.

Another important curriculum decision is: Should alcohol education be incorporated in existing classes or in separate classes? If so, where? Is it a health concern, a chemical discussion for science, a social problem, or an analysis of free enterprise for business courses? These concerns must be handled by school districts prior to alcohol education attempts. Much of the inconsistency can be avoided by timely discussions and a more universal approach.

A similar concern that needs to be considered is the priority that the subject of alcohol receives wherever it is taught. Usually alcohol education receives rather low priority. This low priority is reflected in the lack of support, minimal, if any, course guidance, and a philosophy of the course as a necessary evil to fulfill requirements.

Low priority is also reflected by the manner in which some teachers are "drafted" to teach the subject. Simply having the course taught becomes more important than who teaches it. This overrides the idea that the teacher may be the single most important factor in alcohol education. The school systems will need to decide if they actually value alcohol education or merely value saying that they do. Lack of information and resources and in-service training will hinder the teacher of alcohol education.

CHILDREN NEED TO TALK

The aim of verbalization is to provide opportunities for children to express and ventilate their feelings about their alcoholic parents, their nonalcoholic parents, and alcoholism in general. It is an opportunity to release pent up shame, guilt, fears, and confusion in order to arrive at an impression of parental alcoholism's effect on the individual child.

Getting a child to verbalize may not be easy. It cannot be assumed that the child will want to talk—particularly one whose faith in adults may have been inhibited by painful past experiences with adults. Verbal communication is often tentative for the children of the alcoholic (Hecht, 1977) because children of alcoholics often rely heavily on environmental feedback for a sense of being. Positive environmental feedback can be supplied by the school, but a teacher must realize that in addition to lacking trust in adults, such children may be totally devoid of positive attitudes toward anyone in a position of authority. Feelings of estrangement and powerlessness govern the child who is in an alienated state.

Adding to the difficulty of verbalizing is the fact that such children generally consider discussion of the home situation as "taboo." They may have been ordered by a nonalcoholic parent not to discuss the matter with anyone.

They may have been told that nothing is wrong, but perceive that something is, but do not know how to define it. Also, teachers must understand that children may be ashamed and embarrassed to discuss their home situation. Consequently, the teacher's approach should be matter-of-fact and friendly, but not overly-sympathetic; for above all, these children seldom want pity.

Once a teacher gains the confidence of the child and verbalization occurs, the rewards can be enormous. The greatest benefit (and the primary benefit of verbalization) may not be derived from solving any problems, but merely from "letting the dam burst." Satisfaction and relief can be gained from just sharing or releasing emotions.

At this point, the teacher must remember that his or her role is best served by concentrating on and staying with the feelings of the child. This is not the time to talk about dealing with the alcoholic parent. Nor should judgement be passed on what the child reveals. Such a child has experienced enough negative aspects of the situation, and a great deal of positive or neutral acceptance is needed. In early dialogue with a teacher, the student is apt to be confused about his or her situation and will appreciate encouragement in finding words to share long-inhibited feelings and confidences.

But identifying these children and revealing their problems is just the beginning. With tact and empathy, a skillful teacher can do much to help the child gain a positive self-concept. Gaining trust and confidence will not only open the "family secret," but will also make available to the child an important source of security—a responsible, interested adult.

THE STUDENT'S IDENTITY

Children of alcoholics need to be able to see themselves apart from alcoholism. Assisting them in realizing that they are entitled to lives of their own (self-realization) can be part of the school's function. Schools offer many opportunities for children to achieve self-realization, as well as concerned adults who are able to convey a sense of self-realization to children.

Self-realization is closely associated with the idea of self-concept—amount of belief in one's own abilities. It is not necessary to elaborate upon the relationship between self-concept and academic achievement; one has only to read hundreds of articles and research findings. Obviously, developing a positive self-concept can facilitate a child's achieving self-realization. Often a child may be so absorbed in his or her situation that little or no self-realization is developed, because individual family roles and achievements have been overshadowed by the presence of alcoholism. It becomes important for the teacher to steer discussion away from home problems and to center it on the children and their feelings. The teacher should emphasize that children's feelings are not only important, but natural. A teacher can—and should—convey to children that it is acceptable for them to be concerned about themselves.

The child need not be an extension of the alcoholic. The school is a community and the student is a citizen of that community. Feeling a part of the community can do much to enhance a child's perception that he or she has a role other than living with an alcoholic.

THE RELATIONSHIPS OF STUDENTS

The most important opportunity that the school can provide for children of alcoholic parents is that of developing positive primary relationships. Some children of alcoholics will already have strong primary relationships. These have been designated in the "have" category and they tend to function fairly well, due to the fact that the impact of alcoholism on their lives is being somewhat neutralized by

their relationships with others. Many "haves" are extremely self-sufficient, possess a high degree of self-discipline,
receive high demands on performance from their parents,
or feel that approved academic and/or social performance
will give them a position of family status. With the inter-
nalization of these attributes plus the support of primary
relationships, they may be better equipped to meet the
challenges of the school than children from nonalcoholic
families. These children, who have the most going for them,
will successfully survive both the home situation and
school.

Children who can benefit most from a school program are those who do not possess primary relationships.
In school, opportunities for interaction with others are
greatest and an aware teacher can encourage maximum involvement. Most schools have extensive extracurricular
activities which can provide the foundations for a high degree of personal contact, and at the same time, help students achieve self-realization. Some children only need encouragement to join a club, try out for a team, or volun-
teer their services. Other children may be reluctant, since
they see membership in any organization as an added responsibility and feel that the responsibility of their home
life is enough. In these instances, the teacher may not want
to recommend maximum involvement at the outset. Start-
ing with involvement that is partial or of short duration,

might be better, such as seasonal activity. Exposure to others is the desired initial effect, and the student may make a decision later to accept added activities.

For some students, interaction with a teacher may represent the possibility of a primary relationship. In this role, the teacher must be alert to value judgements. It is necessary to maintain a teacher-student relationship and not to internalize the situation of the student. The role of the teacher should be one of "detached warmth." The teacher's attitudes convey: "I want to help you. I will assist you. I can refer you. But I cannot do it for you." The teacher becomes the guide to a path of self-realization, not the creator of it.

REFERRALS

The final area of service for the school and the teacher is to become a source of referral. No teacher can teach all things to all students. If a program is to be successful, it is essential to know what resources are available for the assistance of children of alcoholics. Alcohol Information Services are available in most communities. For areas lacking local services, a list of national organizations is furnished in the *Appendices* of this book.

Contacting and using local services will be discussed
in Chapter Five, *The Administrators.* Referrals should not
be limited, however, to agencies specializing in alcoholism.
Some referrals may be made within the school itself—such
as advice that the child join a certain club or seek information from another teacher. Students may relate to some
teachers better than to others. The teacher who first learns
of a student's problems may not be the one the student
prefers for communication or assistance.

Knowing the resources is one thing, using them is another. Most local agencies are willing to come to a school
and offer assistance or information; but they seldom do so
unless made aware that their services are needed. A guest
speaker whose talk is followed by an informal question
and answer session is one beneficial service provided free
of charge by most agencies concerned with alcohol education.

IDENTIFYING
CHILDREN OF ALCOHOLIC PARENTS

There are no specific criteria for easy identification of
children whose parents are alcoholics. In fact, many of the
behaviors of such children are similar to those stemming

from other kinds of family problems or situations. The teacher must be able to observe symptomatic behavior patterns and rely on intuition. These patterns will be what will help to distinguish between children of alcoholic parents and other types of problems manifested by children. Aggressive behavior and "acting out" constitute only one behavior pattern that should be noticed. Although some children of alcoholics will indeed act out, others may exhibit patterns of withdrawal or defensiveness.

It is important to remember that individual or single behavioral acts do not constitute behavioral patterns. The teacher must be careful not to jump to conclusions or label children too quickly. The important aspect in identifying these children is the development of patterns, which may either appear in an obvious fashion or require astute observation to discern them. Some behavior patterns which might indicate alcoholism in the student's home are described in the following paragraphs.

Appearance

The overall appearance of a child may reflect his or her home situation. As the home environment fluctuates, so does the child's appearance. The patterns of appearance may reflect the drinking patterns of the alcoholic parent.

If a young child comes to school in an overall untidy condition (dirty clothes, torn apparel, or lacking in personal hygiene), parental indifference or neglect are suggested. This may show itself in a pattern if the child's dress and appearance change from one day to another. If Mondays are particularly "sloppy" days, perhaps the weekend home environment is less than adequate.

Also, the physical condition of the child may indicate physical abuse in the home. The relationship between alcoholic parents and child abuse is unfortunately high. Physical education teachers, school health personnel, coaches, and any other school employee who consistently notices bruises on a child should report it to an administrator. Children who are consistently or frequently bruised should be watched carefully. Also, children who frequently offer excuses so as not to partake in physical education may be doing so in order to avoid the exposure of a physical condition.

Academic Performance

Sporadic variation in academic performance is a key indicator of sporadic variation in a child's home circumstances. A student may perform well when the home situation is calm and do poorly when the home situation is in shambles. Fluctuating academic performance is noticeable to an alert teacher who begins to see regular patterns in the student's periods of achievement and nonachievement, apparently without noticeable reason. Sometimes children from alcoholic homes exhibit better academic performance on certain days of the week, or during certain times of the month. In some, such a pattern may even show itself during certain times of each day. Many children who are concerned about going home may perform well all day and then do poorly or lose attentiveness during the last class of the day.

Report Cards

Parental report card signatures may develop a certain pattern. A familiar pattern for children of alcoholics may be that one parent signs the report card on the occasions it is returned on time, and that the other parent signs the card when it is returned late. Although this may be a minor point, it can serve as a clue when other patterns are present that might suggest alcoholism. The nonalcoholic parent may sign the report card whether both parents have seen it or not. However, if the alcoholic parent was too inebriated to look at or understand the report card, the nonalcoholic may decide to wait for him or her to see it. Since this waiting period may mean returning it late, the alcoholic will usually be asked to sign it since it was he or she who caused the waiting.

Whenever a report card reflects drastic change in a student's performance, either positive or negative, the teacher might ask the child how it was received at home and get a reply to the effect that it was little noticed. This reply, if accompanied by negative "body language," indicates disappointment in parental concern and may be indicative of severe home problems.

Peers

Since some children of alcoholics will already have good primary relationships with others, those without friends may be the most noticeable. Children who are too silent in class, walk by themselves in the hallways, and are otherwise constant "loners" demonstrate symptoms of social disengagement. Also, a child may have only one or two friends who inadvertently mention such things as, "Carol is sad because things are not too good at home." Such clues should be considered by her teachers.

In some situations children of alcoholics are ostracized and avoided by other children. Sometimes (in cases where a parent has engaged in public drunkenness) children are made the brunt of ignorant jokes. Also, some children from "normal" homes may be warned by their parents against associating with them; others may repeat gossip overheard at home. It is little wonder under such conditions that many children from alcoholic homes often voluntarily avoid contact with other children. They are loners by force, not by choice.

At the other extreme are children of alcoholics who, like other children, try to compensate for being ignored at home by demanding excessive attention in school. Such children may be said to be "acting out." The attention these children get from teachers usually consists of various types of punishment. However, teachers should be alert to recognize possible underlying environmental causes of attention seeking behavior. Being the "class clown" may be one method of trying to establish valued relationships with peers when one is starved for attention at home. A poor academic performer may find that by entertaining others, he or she attains some value to others in being at school. It becomes easier for such a person to stay in school. It is their way of coping with a poor school situation.

In summary, the following lists of behaviors may be indicative of children of alcoholics in the school setting (Deutsch, 1982).

General Indications:

- Morning tardiness (especially Monday mornings).

- Consistent concern with getting home promptly at the end of a day or activity period.
- Malodorousness.
- Improper clothing for the weather.
- Regression: thumbsucking, enuresis, infantile behavior with peers.
- Scrupulous avoidance of arguments and conflict.
- Friendlessness and isolation.
- Poor attendance.
- Frequent illness and need to visit nurse, especially for stomach complaints.
- Fatigue and listlessness.
- Hyperactivity and inability to concentrate.
- Sudden temper and other emotional outbursts.
- Exaggerated concern with achievement and satisfying authority in children who are already at the head of the class.
- Extreme fear about situations involving contact with parents.

Indications During Alcohol Education:

- Extreme negativism about alcohol and all drinking.
- Inability to think of healthy, integrative reasons and styles of drinking.
- Equation of drinking with getting drunk.
- Greater familiarity with different kinds of drinks than peers.
- Inordinate attention to alcohol in situations in which it is marginal, for example, in a play or movie not about drinking.
- Normally passive child or distracting child becomes active or focused during alcohol discussions.
- Changes in attendance patterns during alcohol education activities.
- Frequent requests to leave the room.
- Lingering after activity to ask innocent question or simply to gather belongings.
- Mention of parent's drinking to excess on occasion.
- Mention of drinking problem of friend's parent, uncle, or aunt.
- Strong negative feelings about alcoholics.

● Evident concern with whether alcoholism can be inherited.

The various types of coping behaviors mentioned here are not significant when they occur infrequently or individually, but they often contribute to particular difficulties for children of alcoholics. Therefore, it is of considerable importance that students whose parents are alcoholics be identified for help. The next step is to gain the trust and confidence of these students.

In the case of children of alcoholic parents, gaining their trust can be an especially difficult task, since they may have few bonds with adults, even fewer with teachers, and, in fact, may regard the entire school situation as being devoid of any significant bonds. The school may enter their lives, but be viewed with resignation or cynicism and hostility, even if not overtly expressed. Students who view school as a poor place to be and must add this to their problems at home, experience considerable frustration. The source of this frustration may be particularly difficult to ascertain by the student. the student may blame his or her academic inadequacies or the school.

On the other hand, the student who leads a turbulent home life may find the school as a place of rest, a place where he or she is able to maintain a low profile and escape the traumas of family living. The school, for many children of alcoholics, can be the place for rest from home life with little in the way of desired learning taking place. For other students of alcoholics, school may be the place where considerable personal, social, and intellectual attainments occur while being rested from the fatigue acquired at home. In other words, school can be more than a sanctuary for children of alcoholics—it can be a place where they are helped. This is especially true if the students whose parents are alcoholic are recognized.

Therefore, educators should be alert to the behavioral symptoms common in children of alcoholics. After students whose parents are alcoholics are recognized, the school can more effectively utilize its resources in order to achieve for these children growth in attitudes, values, skills, and knowledge.

STUDENT ASSISTANT PROGRAM

Many of the problems for children of alcoholics discussed in this chapter can be addressed in a student assistance program. This type of program will not only serve students in troubled homes, but will also help educators to do their jobs more effectively. The student assistance program usually focuses on students in four categories: (1) students who are children of alcoholics; (2) students who have a substance abuse problem; (2) students who are children of alcoholics and have a substance abuse problem; and (4) students who have neither an alcoholic parent nor a substance abuse problem, but have other problems.

Personnel for the development and maintenance of a student assistance program could come from concerned school personnel, students and community resources such as an alcoholism treatment facility or a community mental health association (Westchester County Department of Community Mental Health, 1981).

Read. Read Read 6 Read

: NOTE :

I told my mom about you speakers
I told her about the things
it could do My Mom is
an Alcoholic I convinced her
into going to the State Hospital
she is going I THANK YOU

VERY MUCH FOR COMING
TO OUR SCHOOl.

Read

One of several letters written to the author by a student in the eighth
grade class at Watson Junior High School, Colorado Springs, Colorado.

5

The Administrators

A deservable program that meets the needs of students with alcoholic parents will be mutually supported by school administrators and their staffs. They will work together. The entire staff will be able to recognize and be sensitive to the symptoms and problems of coming from an alcoholic home. The staff will also be familiar with resources that are available to them for achieving their objective of helping children of alcoholics. Of course, the accomplishment of any successful school objective depends to a considerable extent on the supervisory roles of administrators as they work to mutually involve teachers and other staff in the planning and implementation of activities.

Until recently, many administrators have hesitated to get involved in focusing on children of alcoholics, asking, "Is this an issue that really concerns the school?" Obviously, the family problems of all children have educational implications; children of alcoholics are no different than others in this regard.

Furthermore, the school's role is to work with students and not to work with the alcoholic problems of the parents of students. However, the school should work with students who have alcoholic parents so that they may develop the same kinds of personal and social strengths that are advocated for all students.

It is possible that some will feel a need to question the legality of taking into account family conditions such as alcoholism when planning educational programs. On the other hand, since the overall purpose of a sound program to help children of alcoholics is to help them attain the same goals as are held for all students, and neither the students nor their parents will be subjected to an inquisition regarding drinking habits, it is doubtful that legal difficulties will emerge. However, should educators find themselves heading toward legal problems, the nature of their involvement with parents and students should be quickly reassessed.

Even if there are no legal problems, the question of taking into account alcoholic conditions in the family may, nonetheless, bring up ethical or moral concerns. The position may be taken by some that alcoholic parents are strictly a family problem, and that any problems which result at school because of home conditions are entirely a family matter; the family is the only one responsible. However, we know that the school and family are not that separate in their influence; actually they greatly affect each other. Furthermore, many attempts are constantly going on to ameliorate poor conditions at home. Many lunch programs and other compensatory education programs have been developed to help children overcome the difficulties of background. The same kinds of needs are there for others. In fact, by federal and state law, the schools are now concerned about child abuse and neglect at home.

However, if the schools are going to efficiently take into account the rather unique problems of students, including those whose parents are alcoholic, then the leadership of school administrators becomes crucial. There are four areas, among others, that the leadership skills of administrators should initially focus upon. They are: 1) in-service training, 2) development of resources, 3) policy support, and 4) program coordination. Effective educational leadership in these four areas can become the catalyst for development and maintenance of a successful program.

IN-SERVICE TRAINING

The area of staff in-service training is a vital function for all schools, since at these sessions up-to-date techniques and issues can be brought forth. In an effective program

for students with alcoholic parents, in-service training
should fulfill several goals.

One objective of in-service training should be to sensitize school staff to the presence of students with special
problems stemming from alcoholic conditions at home.
The staff needs to become aware of what alcoholism is and
is not and its impact on families. A second objective should
be to deal with questions about what teachers and other
school staff should and should not do in working with children of alcoholics. A third aim of in-service programs should
be to provide alcohol education materials and suggestions
for what the school staff can do in a variety of situations
at school. Topics to explore during in-service training should
cover various methods for getting students to be more
aware of their own potential, to be able to better express
their feelings, and to be more clear about their values.
There are many communication techniques and exercises
in the areas of value clarification and group dynamics
which can facilitate discussion and provide vehicles to self-
expression and self-awareness for children of alcoholics, as
well as others.

In-service training need not be limited to the subjects
of alcohol, alcoholism, or the children of alcoholic parents.
It is not necessary to dwell upon the topic of alcohol. The
real benefits of in-service training will be derived from
developing some practical guidelines for the school for its

own philosophy and procedural arrangements to meet the needs of its children from alcoholic homes.

In-service training on the subject of children of alcoholic parents must be followed up. Assuming that the first few sessions have been able to sensitize personnel, it becomes imperative that sessions be arranged for discussions and guidelines after real situations have been encountered. Asking teachers or other school personnel to become aware of a situation without providing avenues of feedback and growth is often self-defeating; it may in fact increase levels of teacher frustration of inadequacy, since recognition of a problem can become very taxing if the means to solve it are not made available.

DEVELOPMENT OF RESOURCES

Most communities fall under a county or state program for substance abuse which is normally affiliated with the county or state health department. These programs can help with in-service training, loan or recommendation of films and publications, and the providing of guest speakers. Administrators may want to seek advice from a substance abuse agency to explore ideas and alternative methods. Some communities have several programs working in the area of alcohol and drug rehabilitation, all of which are eager to furnish assistance in setting up and maintaining school services to children of alcoholics.

Many programs and agencies at the national level can also provide access to excellent resource materials. Time and effort in finding materials can be reduced by corresponding with national agencies, specifying the type of program, and asking for assistance and materials. However, face-to-face contact with local persons, rather than national speakers, should be utilized whenever possible in order to fit the individual needs of the school.

At the national level is an organization called Alateen. This is a group solidarity-based organization operating very similarly to Al-Anon, which is an organization for the nonalcoholic spouses of alcoholics. Members of Alateen are children of alcoholic parents, and the basic purpose of Alateen is to help such children appreciate or understand their identities. It also explores the plight of the alcoholic and possible ways of helping or at least coping with an alcoholic parent. The benefits of this organization can be considerable since children in each group are able, in settings of confidentiality, to share a problem they all have in common. A better understanding of parents, a better self-concept, and increased self-confidence usually result. By corresponding with the national Alateen organization, one can obtain information about Alateen meetings in their areas, or get advice on how to ask the local Al-Anon chapter to start one of these groups for youngsters in your area.

Although Alateen is not formally affiliated with or sponsored by any specific organization, it utilizes various public facilities for meetings. The school building could be an excellent place to start a new chapter, however, it should *not* be officially sponsored by the school.

Another resource for all kinds of help that may be effectively utilized is Alcoholics Anonymous. Although anonymity is a characteristic of the organization, there are many recovering alcoholics who are willing to speak openly on the subject. Many recovering alcoholics are parents themselves and would welcome the opportunity to become involved in a school program. This can usually be arranged through the local resources or a call to the local AA chapter. In many communities, AA membership and its power are seldom comprehended by the general public. AA is one of the best resources available to a school: a "people" resource rich in experience.

Additional community resources that are often found beneficial are social organizations and agencies working with family problems, child abuse, child guidance, and self-help of various kinds. Many communities contain a college or university that offers courses in family and substance abuse, from which a willing instructor might be utilized for in-service training.

There are many resources available at the local, state, federal, and national level which can be helpful in developing programs for children of alcoholics. The appendix contains agency addresses and suggested resources that can be beneficial to a school program for children of alcoholics.

The key to successful resource utilization is to take advantage of every available means.

POLICY SUPPORT

Any program to assist children of alcoholic parents needs to be supported if it is to be successful; and, like in-service training, support must be followed up to be successful. Follow-up will allow for the ironing out of initial policy problems and helps to shape the eventual direction of the program.

A school's policy on a program of this nature can be formal or informal. Specific guidelines and policy statements will be utilized in a formal program, whereas informal programs will operate in a less structured manner. The amount of formalization will depend partially upon prevailing attitudes in a district. Attitudes are generally influenced by the community's tolerance of the use of alcohol, and certainly the drinking patterns of those making the decisions will have an impact.

In the development of school policy, the role of the school is supporting children—while avoiding direct involvement in the problems of their alcoholic parents—and must be completely understood by everyone. It should also be clear that such a program is not the same as alcohol education—even though alcohol education may be in the curriculum, and used as an aid in identifying children of alcoholics. A program to help the children of alcoholic parents is not a matter of curriculum development alone. It is a question of using the positive aspects of the community and school atmosphere to assist in the growth of children who need support and guidance outside their home environment.

Another aspect of policy support is monetary. In-service training, guest speakers, and the purchase of reference materials will take some money and time of staff; however, it is doubtful that such costs will be excessive. Materials can be obtained from various agencies at little or no cost. Nevertheless, it is usually necessary to have some monetary arrangements initiated by the school administrator for incidental expenses such as film rental or acquisition of special materials.

PROGRAM COORDINATION

Critical to the overall success of a program for children of alcoholics will be the coordination of the various aspects of the program. This will involve not only the managing of the program within the school, but also within the community.

At the school level, decisions will need to be made regarding how the program will operate, who is involved, and their level of involvement. Admistrators may want to coordinate these activities themselves or delegate an individual or group for these responsibilities. Programs will achieve more success if a single source of information is available, such as a resource room for information material, knowing who is in charge of what phase, and the role or roles of school personnel in the program. Knowing whom to go to will enhance cooperation and involvement by school personnel.

Coordination outside of school will include establishing rapport with local resource personnel and building community support for the program. Also, existing community programs for students will provide additional alternatives for working with children of alcoholics. These programs could include other types of self-help groups, as well as opportunities for recreational group membership.

The goal of coordination will be to keep sections of the school program from becoming fragmented or isolated. Substantial interaction within as well as outside of the program is necessary for success. Not only will this enhance program effectiveness, but it will also provide avenues of feedback regarding the strong and weak aspects of the program.

SUMMARY

The mutual support of all school personnel is a must if a program to help students of alcoholic parents is to have a chance at success. The responsibility for this support will belong to all school employees, but it will be much easier for a program to succeed if it is actively endorsed by school administrators.

Raising the level of awareness of the plight of students from alcoholic homes will not be enough. Guidelines for help, establishment of resources, and involvement with these students is necessary. All of these endeavors will require support and coordination.

6

Outside of the Classroom

All educators can help children of alcoholics. Regardless of whether you are a teacher, school nurse, counselor, social worker, librarian, club advisor, or director of a school activity, you will have many opportunities to help students with home problems. If you take advantage of your opportunities, there are at least three things you can do to help those who have a parent who is an alcoholic.

The first thing that you can do is to be an effective listener and communicator. This means that you should help your students to be able to express their feelings and thereby deal with their fears and aspirations. One of the more unfortunate problems experienced by some children of alcoholics is that they have no one to talk with about their needs, fears, and hopes.

A second thing that you can do for students of alcoholics is to facilitate their skills in developing needed primary relationships with other students and adults. Some children of alcoholics have a difficult time in relating to their peers and adults. Like all students, they need opportunities to participate with others in primary group activities. However, many children of alcoholics need supportive counseling to be effective in using group activities to foster needed primary group relationships.

The third opportunity that you should not miss when it avails itself is to carefully observe your students and their situations. What you observe can be essential to being of assistance to them. Counselors, school nurses and coaches often have a special advantage in being able to observe conditions about which the student, their families, or other professionals very much need to know.

LISTENING AND COMMUNICATING

Counselors and school social workers typically have responsibilities for listening, advising, counseling, and sometimes providing therapy to students. In part, others also share these roles. While it is not a formal requirement that coaches and club advisors act as counselors, they may act in ways consonant with good counseling. Within certain restrictions, every educator should help students to talk about what they like and dislike about their lives. However, it is important to know when assistance from other professionals is necessary. In this regard, each educator needs to have knowledge of his or her own competencies and limitations.

Know Your Limitations

Of course, all professional staff will need to consider their legal, ethical and professional obligations as well as their competencies in deciding what they should and should not do with students. It is very important that educators seek assistance in areas where they are not authorized to function. If they are not trained as therapists, they should not try and act as therapists. If there is any doubt about the severity of a student's personal or social problems, there are usually counselors, school psychologists or school social workers available who will gladly offer their assistance.

When Talking with Students

Of course, the need for you does not cease after a student reveals to you that he or she has an alcoholic parent. Rather, the need for effective educators is intensified. It is often after confiding about one's problem that the benefits of interacting with others occurs most.

A viable concern at this point may be how the parents will react to their child's confiding in someone outside the family. Will an irate alcoholic parent come to school complaining that you have interfered in their family's private business? However, if you limit your discussions with students to the student's feelings and to an understanding of what alcoholism is, there probably will be no cause for parent concern. Furthermore, if care is taken to avoid communicating that the student's difficulties are those of his or her parent's alcoholism and you direct attention to the student's school and social performance, the parent is very likely to welcome your help.

As a sidelight, the expression of denial of any drinking related problems is deemed important by those alcoholic parents who want to continue drinking. Similarly, the spouse of an alcoholic may have his or her felt need to refrain from talking about drinking related difficulties. Consequently, in parent contacts it is probable that alcoholism will not be a matter for discussion. And if the topic comes up, perhaps you should remain silent on the subject of the parent's drinking.

In the exploration of peer relationships with either the parents or their children, there are several factors to consider. The benefits of getting students involved in extracurricular activities have already been mentioned. Another suggestion is to foster situations whereby certain children of alcoholic parents can become involved with one another. Since one of the problems in working with students who have an alcoholic parent is inducing them to "open up," it may be easier for them to talk with their peers who have similar experiences than it is for them to confide in an adult.

Group activities and discussions can be especially effective with teenagers since they are in an age bracket where they are adopting new values. One value that is fostered in youth groups appears to be a concern for each others' welfare. It may be a good idea to have the students consider calling each other at home when times are bad. They can use the mutual support of their peers in maintaining their poise and compassion.

If a student discussion group is formed, it should not be identified as being focused upon alcohol problems. Moreover, since there are many types of family problems affecting educational outcomes, such a group may take on any number of organizational themes and objectives. Such themes as "understanding your parents better" may be employed. A general approach would also reduce any embarrassment at being involved in an activity that is known for dealing with certain home problems. Also, since the primary purpose of a group discussion should be to meet student's needs, an organizational theme dealing with "self-awareness" and examining personal feelings may be appropriate.

If group discussion appears to be too formal or stigmatizing, a "walk-in center" for students may prove workable. A walk-in center can serve as a multiple program for students meeting various needs by dealing not only with home life, but with their many other problems. Such a center would be an obvious place for not only activities and discussions, but also as a place where they can obtain information on a variety of subjects ranging from alcohol and drug use to whatever else concerns them.

Remember, whatever the activity that is fostered, at all times it must be clear that the purpose of group discussions and walk-in centers should be to assist students; they should not attempt changes in the students' home environments.

In attempting to establish group interactions, it should also be kept in mind that many children of alcoholics find it difficult to make new friends. Many are very withdrawn or complete loners. The professional educator may be aware of the benefits to be derived from peer relationships, but their skills will be put to a test to prove such benefits to a student who has never had friends. They must also be prepared to be helpful when something goes wrong, after a student takes advice to seek friendship. Perhaps the student has confided in someone who did not understand, or worse yet, subjected the student to ridicule.

Perhaps your greatest contribution will be in the areas of helping students to discover that their feelings are normal and that it is normal to be confused and sometimes upset about their home environments. Exploring students'

feelings with them can help you obtain a better understanding of them. More importantly, exploration of feelings may allow students to grown in self-understanding.

FACILITATING PRIMARY RELATIONSHIPS

School personnel who lead extracurricular activities
have many opportunities to assist in the establishment of
primary relationships for students who are children of alcoholic parents. Like others, these students can acquire
many benefits from extracurricular activities. However,
for children of alcoholics, the more obvious benefits of
extracurricular activities may be secondary to the benefits
achieved through establishment and maintenance of peer
relationships. The students not only learn how to take part
in a sport, publish a newspaper, etc., but also gain a sense
of belonging and roles that they value.

A vital role that you can have in the case of children
of alcoholic parents is in getting them involved. However,
recruiting children of alcoholics into group activities may
be more difficult than directing them once they join. This
is true because many such students are not eager to join
school groups. This is particularly true if they feel that an
extracurricular activity is just another responsibility to
endure, rather than a vehicle by which they can reduce the

strain of existing responsibilities. Furthermore, when a student's feelings of self-worth are minimal, he or she may feel incapable of contributing anything to a group and may have to be persuaded that his or her participation is needed.

Nonclassroom activities can also serve to reduce the time spent by children of alcoholic parents in uncomfortable situations. This is very desirable in itself. More importantly, however, extracurricular activities provide more time and opportunities for such children to interact with you and other potential adult role models. In addition, some students may feel that an educator outside of the classroom is more approachable than a teacher within a classroom, or that it is more permissible to discuss "after school" matters after school.

MAKING OBSERVATIONS

When you are with students, of course, you need to be very observant if you are to help them in achieving an understanding of their conditions. Your observations may focus on their peer relationships, academic interests, achievements, reasons for talking to you about their problems, willingness to share attitudes and confidences, and their evaluations of their home situation. This last concern will probably be difficult for you to explore and may depend more in the beginning on how they act than on what they say.

When you are near students, there are a number of things about which you should be sensitive. Among these are physically observable symptoms which may reflect serious home problems, such as chronic fatigue, confusion, or emotional strain. Although all educators should be sensitive to these symptoms, health care professionals can play an especially vital role in making valid observations of students who are suspected of having health related problems which stem from their home life.

Because of their focused interest and training in health, nurses and physical activity directors can detect subtle details of a student's appearance beyond those of obvious bruises that might suggest parental abuse or neglect. Bruises concealed by clothing can come under their scrutiny. Also, students suffering symptoms of strain are usually more noticeable to health workers than others. Health workers are also aware of students who have frequent headaches, high levels of anxiety, and constant fatigue.

However, if child abuse or neglect is suspected, the law in all fifty states requires immediate referral of the student in question to an appropriate child protection agency. In no way should an educator question a child or a child's parents in regard to abuse or neglect without the involvement and support of the child protection agency.

Besides obvious physical abuse and neglect, educators will want to take into account periods of excessive fatigue or student strain and particularly when these symptoms occur. As with other identifying concerns, these symptoms may be more obvious on certain days than on others. These occurrences of fatigue, etc., may show a pattern, and it is the development of particular patterns of times of strain that should be observed the most. For children of alcoholic parents, these patterns are likely to reflect the occurrence of conflict within the home. For example, if an alcoholic parent is a chronic weekend drinker, every Monday may be manifested in the child falling asleep in class or being very listless. On Tuesdays through Thursdays the student may appear to be somewhat energetic, and on Friday exhibit high levels of tension at the thought of the coming weekend. Of course, different patterns can occur, and if your in-service program on children of alcoholic parents includes trained workers in alcoholism, they will be able to alert you to many symptoms of living in a family with alcoholism.

It is important that you be constantly alert to the needs of your students. If you are accurate in your observations, you will be able to be of considerable help to them in both how you behave and how you affect others in their actions. When talking with parents and professional colleagues, your accurate assessments of students may allow you to better inform them about what they can do and when referral is needed.

PART C

SUGGESTIONS FOR THERAPISTS AND PARENTS

7

Implications for Therapists

Therapists working with children of alcoholics should be especially concerned that their clients are able to establish positive relations with others and that they have confidence in their own abilities and worth. In order to help clients who have a parent who is an alcoholic to overcome personal inadequacies in these areas, three critical areas may need to be considered. These areas involve conditions for effecting positive relationships with others, ways of reducing feelings of powerlessness, and strategies for resolving conflict.*

---

*Of course, the professional therapist will assess the unique needs of his or her clients prior to attempting treatment. It is also recognized that the methods of treatment a therapist uses are the therapist's responsibility, that no particular type of therapy is suggested here. The purpose of the discussion in this chapter is to describe particular kinds of problems children of alcoholics suffer toward which therapists may need to be especially sensitive.

EFFECTIVE RELATIONSHIPS

One primary concern for the therapist should be the child's ability to develop and maintain quality primary relationships with others. It is quite likely that many children and adolescents who see a therapist will not have desirable relationships with their peers or adults. Many children of alcoholics have the problem of what some therapists refer to as being "socially disengaged;" in other words, their relationships with others are superficial and their contacts with others are often limited in number and intensity. When working with this problem, the therapist will need to be particularly sensitive to assessing the strengths and weaknesses of children of alcoholics as they are currently interacting with others. Whatever relationships therapists find, they will need to use them to build stronger as well as new social alignments for their clients.

Therapists have at their disposal many strategies for assessing the nature of a person's relationships with others. For example, one method of assessing the level of contact of influence others have on children of alcoholics is to use a sociogram. The sociogram is a method of constructing larger and larger circles, each representing different individuals or groups that influence the client with the client as the center of the circle. For example, the client represents the middle circle and the next circle represents "significant others" or those that have the most influence on the client. This circle usually includes the family members or close friends. As succeeding circles are added, each will have less influence on the client. In this manner, the therapist will be able to assess the people and the extent of their influence on the client.

Although the therapist can emphasize developing new relationships, it is usually necessary to examine existing ones with parents, as well as past relationships with parents. Clients may move from a relationship of confusion and love to one of frustration and bitterness. Helping children of alcoholics to interact more positively with their parents is critical. It is one relationship they can seldom escape no matter how old or even if they leave home.

However, the therapist need not be concerned with achieving sobriety in the client's parents or focusing on changing parents. The therapist who is only working with the client and not the client's family should be concerned with the physical and emotional survival of the client. A certain amount of the work of the therapist in this situation might be focused on "how to survive with an alcoholic parent." In this vain, getting clients to discuss their feelings about their situation and themselves may be more important than discussions that center on their alcoholic parents. The important thrust is to help the client of an alcoholic help him or herself to have more rewarding and healthy relationships at home with his or her parents and siblings, as well as with others outside the home. In other words, merely surviving in their home environment is not enough.

Other relationships the client of an alcoholic parent has with people outside of his or her family can also provide a support structure for not only the client's survival, but also for the client's growth as a person. Peers can provide many necessary friendships for healthy personal development. Therefore, the therapist may need to give considerable attention to helping some clients who are children of alcoholics with their peer relationships.

For those clients with only a few healthy peer relationships, the therapist may want to concentrate on developing various social skills. For example, some therapists may utilize tasks where the client is helped to attend a number of social functions whereby he or she meets new people. Those clients from alcoholic homes who have low feelings of self-esteem are prone to see themselves as uninteresting and feel that nobody likes to talk with them. If the therapist is able to help the client to develop adequate conceptions of self which are relevant to the various people with whom he or she comes in contact, then the foundation is laid for effective and needed primary relationships with others. The therapist will have to take a major step in helping his or her client survive and grow both outside and inside of their alcoholic home.

FEELINGS OF POWERLESSNESS

Children within an alcoholic home are likely to feel a strong sense of powerlessness. They are likely to see themselves as devoid of resources or ways of alleviating their parent's drinking or fighting. This felt loss of control can be carried over to other areas, including school. Most important, however, is that this sense of powerlessness can be felt to encompass every aspect of their lives. That is, they generally feel powerless over themselves.

In this situation, the therapist is faced with a "there is nothing I can do" attitude. Much of this feeling arises from a lack of an identity they value. Often children of alcoholics fail to see that their achievements can be, to a considerable extent, separate from those of their alcoholic parent. If they cannot influence their alcoholic parent, they wonder how they can help themselves. Therapists need to be sure that their clients establish a sense of valued identity and achievement independent of their identities as children of alcoholics. In this regard, conversations with the clients may need to be directed away from the home environment and more on the client and his or her aspirations and expectations outside of felt family needs.

One strategy in working with children of alcoholics is where the therapist helps the client to recognize that they cannot control the behavior of others whose effects they may have to endure. However, they can learn that they are able to control their own behavior, achievements, and feelings. To the extent that the therapist can help the client to develop a sense of control over his or her life, they facilitate the discovery for that client that he or she is an individual with appropriate and valuable feelings, attributes, and capabilities. In working through feelings of powerlessness, the development of a sense of valued identities can lead to internal resources for clients. These resources can enhance the abilities of the client for determining the outcomes of the behaviors of their alcoholic parents, even though they cannot control their parent's behavior.

In other words, it is important that children of alcoholics, like others, develop a sense of personal responsibility for much of what will happen to them. Unfortunately, all too often children of alcoholics conclude that their unhappiness or happiness is totally the result of others. Whether content or discontent, they perceive an inability to control their lives. The therapist in working with such clients may need to avoid having his or her clients shift from placing all responsibility for their problems on their parents to placing the responsibility for their happiness on them because they are their "therapist."

CONFLICT RESOLUTION

Most therapists believe that meeting the psychological needs of clients may require helping clients to resolve con-

flicts they may experience. One approach to conflict resolution focuses on three types of conflict that may occur.
These are approach-approach conflict, avoidance-avoidance
conflict, and approach-avoidance conflict.

Approach-Approach Conflict

Approach-approach conflict results when two goals
are simultaneously desired, and to reach one goal will
mean not achieving the other. It is common in the alcoholic
home for the children to want to talk about their parent's
drinking, but they also want to have good relationships
with their parents. However, they fear that if they talk
about their parent's drinking with their parents, their relationships with them will suffer. As a result, they may experience conflict within themselves. The force of external
conditions appears to rule their lives. Mechanisms need to
be developed for the expression of any such internal conflict. Without the outlet of expression, the client may be
needlessly forced to endure excessive internal approach-
approach conflict at the expense of many personal needs.

Avoidance-Avoidance Conflict

Avoidance-avoidance conflict is the typical circum-
stance of "you are damned if you do and damned if you
don't." The child in an alcoholic home is likely to feel that

if he or she interferes with the parent's alcoholic behavior that he or she will be sanctioned — in particular, that the parent's love may be lost. Not to interfere, however, means that the undesired drinking related behaviors of the parent will continue. Another typical example in the family of children of alcoholics is where the child is told the alcoholic parent doesn't have a drinking problem, but they are also told not to tell anyone about the parent's drinking habits. If nothing is wrong, why not talk about it?

Approach-Avoidance Conflict

Another form of conflict is the approach-avoidance type which is characterized by mixed feelings. A person is attracted to an object, but is repulsed by some component of it. The child of an alcoholic tends to love the alcoholic parent rather intensely, while simultaniously hating the drinking. The resolution of this type of conflict may be the most challenging for a therapist. If the child is able to overcome the distinction between the parent as an alcoholic and as a parent with many qualities other than those of being alcoholic, then the client may be able to see him or herself with many attributes other than those of being a member of an alcoholic home.

FAMILY ISSUES

In addition to the problem areas already mentioned, a therapist is likely to be faced with assisting the child of an alcoholic understand and resolve some of the following issues (Morehouse, 1982):

- Worrying about the health of the alcoholic parent.
- Being upset and angry by the unpredictable and inconsistent behavior of the alcoholic parent and the lack of support from the nonalcoholic parent.
- Worrying about fights and arguments between their parents.
- Being scared and upset by the violence or possibility of violence in their family.
- Being upset by the parent's inappropriate behavior which can include criminal or sexual behavior.
- Being disappointed by broken promises and feeling unloved.
- Feeling responsible for their parents drinking.

The resolution of these concerns can best be treated through integrative family therapy.

Integrative Family Therapy

Family therapy is a goal. Integrative family therapy is beginning therapy with those individuals needing and wanting help first and then later integrating them with other family members. In this manner family therapy uses a building-block approach, attempting to build from a single family member toward the integration of others. In the event that other members of a family are unwilling to join, at least the needs of one are met. This one person who needs help and is willing to confront the alcoholism is often the child of the alcoholic. Even though it would be desirable for the entire family to enter into treatment, this is seldom the case. The therapist working with the child of the alcoholic may never have the "luxury" of working with the entire family. Certainly this form of family therapy has its limitations, but it is not as limiting as total avoidance of the family. It should also be noted that integrative family therapy is not limited to the integration of family members with each other. It also includes integrating the children with outside community activities, friends and extended family.

SUMMARY

Helping children of alcoholics to work through their feelings and establish effective relationships with others will be very helpful in overcoming the impact of an alcoholic parent. Moreover, the therapist will be helpful if he or she is able to assist such children in developing confidence in themselves. Clients need to believe that they can control how they feel about what is happening in their lives. They need to know that they can influence what is going to happen. If able to develop this self-confidence, the therapist's success will be far more reaching than that of just helping a client to survive while in an alcoholic home. The long-range effects may mean that the client will not become one of the forty to sixty percent of children of alcoholics who become alcoholics themselves.

8

Recommendations for Concerned Parents

Whether you or your spouse have a drinking problem, your children are affected. This is true for your children who are still at home and for those that are on their own. This chapter examines recommendations for parents who want to help reduce detrimental consequences for their children resulting from exposure to parental alcoholism. Although sobriety for the alcoholic parent is the best beginning to a solution for alcoholism, not all alcoholics will become sober. Unfortunately, the number of alcoholics who continue drinking outnumber those who stop drinking. Furthermore, alcoholism recovery is not an instant process. It can take years to work through the denial phase before seeking help. Once in treatment, the family will find that the treatment itself is also time consuming. To simply wait for sobriety delays or totally negates efforts to help your children. While waiting for sobriety, marriages can physically or emotionally fall apart, children grow up and leave home, and family members become resigned to quiet desperation. The alternative is to do something and to do it—NOW.

Although desirable, it is not necessary nor a prerequisite for the alcoholic parent to seek help before beginning to help the children of the family. The alcoholic as well as the nonalcoholic parent can be of help to the children. Even though the alcoholic continues drinking, this does not mean that he or she does not want the best for the children. The alcoholic has lost the ability to control his or her drinking, but this does not mean that he or she has lost the ability to care about his or her children. What is in jeopardy for both parents is the ability to openly express these feelings. In the alcoholic family much energy is absorbed in surviving alcoholic behavior and there is usually little energy left for other relationships. When families become entrenched in this survival mode, two necessary ingredients for healthy family relationships become severely diminished: (1) the energy necessary for positive alternatives; and (2) open expressions of feelings of love.

One of the major problems in alcoholic homes is a lack of energy. Existing energy is consumed by daily survival tasks. Little energy remains for exploration of alternatives. Many alcoholic homes are characterized by family members devoid of positive alternatives. The home becomes a "habit cage" and the habit is the repetition of survival behaviors. There is a major difference between "negative survival" and "positive living." If members of the alcoholic family are going to go beyond mere survival they must invest new energy and re-direct existing energy towards positive alternatives in their lives.

One of these alternatives is to openly share feelings and emotions in the home regarding alcoholism and family relationships. As mentioned earlier, however, many feelings are denied so as to avoid injury or they are subjugated for the sake of not rocking the boat. With the withdrawal of feelings comes the feeling of isolation.

YOU ARE NOT ALONE

Being an alcoholic or the spouse of an alcoholic is not a unique situation numerically. There are at least 9.3 to 10 million alcoholics in the United States and most of these are married. It is obvious that many people are affected by alcoholism, but why do so many feel alone?

Much of the feelings of loneliness and uniqueness in the alcoholic family stem from the attempts to cover up the existence of alcoholism within and outside of the home. A self-imposed silence is used to avoid outside detection, but unfortunately it also denies the opportunity for outside help. Within the family, even when members admit and are aware of the alcoholism, they may not be aware of or admit to the need for help either for themselves or for other members of the family. If you deny that a situation exists or that help is needed you are not likely to do anything about it. However, living with an alcoholic has very real consequences and the family that denies this outwardly will still find itself inwardly covering up the alcoholic behavior. There is little doubt that children in such situations have difficulty understanding when they are asked to cover up for something that they have been told to deny. This is particularly true in situations where children ask "Where is Dad?" or "What is wrong with Mom?", only to be told "Nothing is wrong, but do not tell anyone." This parental response is usually an honest attempt by the parent to "protect" the children. This manner of "protection," however, increases isolation within the family because children are not informed about what is happening in their own family.

On the other hand, the alcoholic or nonalcoholic parent may say "I've got to protect the children, I don't want them to know what is happening." In this situation parents are concerned about protecting their children by not letting them become aware of the "real situation." This form of protection seldom works. If your children are capable of observing your behavior, expressions, attitudes and overall disposition, they know when you are concerned and anxious. They may not know the exact details regarding the drinking and sub-sequent behavior, but they know when something is wrong or when one or both parents are upset, drinking or frustrated. What is needed in this instance is not futile attempts at protection, but rather honest efforts to overcome the impact of exposure to alcoholism upon your children. Direct your efforts at helping your children to understand and overcome any detrimental consequences of the alcoholic home. Once they are capable of observing the family dynamics, they are beyond protection and will need your support in recovering from exposure.

Such protection attempts may further contribute to your feelings of being alone. Maintaining silence precludes discussion of the alcoholism and the sharing of feelings, which could help defuse the sense of isolation. Your family is a resource for recovery not a liability contributing to isolation.

A LETTER TO THE NONALCOHOLIC PARENT

Dear Nonalcoholic Parent:

At this point you may have many feelings and concerns about your children ranging from frustration and fear to awareness and hope. However, do not allow yourself to be alone with these feelings and concerns. Can both the alcoholic and the nonalcoholic parent help their children? Yes, even though as you are reading this you might be saying, "No, because I am the one who has to pick up the pieces and hold the family together." At times this is true, but to ignore the alcoholic's parenting responsibilities is to provide further support for his or her drinking. This will only add to your feelings of isolation and aloneness. You may be asking, "Why bother, what's the use?" Maybe in terms of the alcoholic it does appear hopeless, but how about for your children? What about you?

Without any intervention or help, your children stand an exceptionally high probability of becoming alcoholic themselves. They need your help and you too need help and support. It is hoped that the following recommendations will not only offer you alternatives, but also encourage you to take a more active interest in yourself and in your children.

Sincerely,

A LETTER TO THE ALCOHOLIC PARENT

Dear Alcoholic Parent:

Whether or not you consider yourself to be an alcoholic, if your drinking is creating problems for your family, then help is needed. Obviously, a solution to the drinking problem is the best choice of alternatives. However, while approaching this solution, and even often after it has been found, your family will need support.

You might be saying at this point that your drinking is your business and that you are not hurting anyone. If this is true, why did someone you know buy this book?

Your behavior does not go unnoticed by your children. To one degree or another your children are involved with your drinking. Although you can try to ignore someone physically, if you live with them you cannot avoid them emotionally. Lack of participation with you does not mean that your children and spouse are not involved in the "alcoholic game." You may interpret your family's passive resistance as tolerance for your behavior. However, you might ask: "Is it tolerance, a method of survival, embarrassment or disdain?"

How can you help? Be honest with your family. If you do not want to be honest with yourself regarding drinking, at least be open with your children. Do not try to hide what they can see, you are only hiding from communication. They may understand your drinking, but not your silence nor your denial.

While still being an active alcoholic it will be impossible to overcome many of the effects that your drinking has upon your family. However, if you recognize your impact, you can also help to reduce some of its magnitude. Regardless of what you may or may not do with the guidelines in this book, if you love your children—tell them. Do not be afraid to express your feelings of affection. Many times alcoholics withhold their love because they do not feel that it will be accepted. Offer it to your children. In many cases children can still distinguish between you and your behavior. They can still love you, but hate your drinking. Besides, you have little to lose since your present behavior is not receiving the highest level of acceptance either. All children need love, concern, guidance and caring from their parents. Being an alcoholic does not excuse you from giving these nor does it excuse you from your parenting responsibilities. Do not increase the distance between you and your children by silence and avoidance.

Finally, a word of caution. This letter is not intended to contribute to your denial nor to exacerbate your drinking. Nor is it the intention to lead you to believe that this is all that you need to do. You need to get sober! NOW!

Sincerely,

WHAT YOU CAN DO

Much of what parents can do to assist their children to overcome the consequences of their or their spouse's alcoholism will depend upon the conditions present in each family. The following suggestions are offered for both parents even though only one may be alcoholic:

- **Be flexible regarding the demands that you make on yourself and your children remembering that problematic situations call for adaptable measures.**

Often the alcoholic home becomes characterized by a very rigid family system due to attempts to control the situation. However, too much control for your children may be interpreted by them as blaming them for the situation. Remember they did not cause the alcoholism, they are only trying to survive it.

- **Try not to isolate yourself and your family from outside interaction or from interaction within your home.**

Realizing that you want to help and protect your children, you can attempt to insulate them from negative reactions to alcoholism, but do not isolate your children. They will need external supports to help withstand internal conflicts.

- **Do not blame your children for wanting to get help.**

Often parents in the alcoholic home are embarrassed

when their children are being helped. This is your embarrassment, not theirs. Do not be offended that they have
turned to someone else. Professional help is needed in serious
circumstances.

●   **The alcoholic is not to be excused from parenting.**

It is important for children that the alcoholic parent is
still as much a positive part of the family as is possible.
Remember that the alcoholic is still a role model for the
children and they will learn many other behaviors besides
alcoholism from he or she. One of these behaviors will be
the modeling of being a parent.

●   **Avoid pressuring your children, either verbally
     or with your actions, to take sides in conflicts you
     have with your spouse.**

Your children do not need nor do they usually want
to take sides, but rather want you, their parents, to behave

in ways that do not demand their siding with one or the other. If they are forced into taking one parent's side or another, even more problems are forced upon them. Further, pressure upon children to take sides in marital conflicts usually intensifies the conflict for both the husband and wife and the children.

- **Avoid using the opinions of your children about the use of alcohol or the alcoholic parent to get at the alcoholic.**

Using your children against your spouse is like taking sides and places them in a vulnerable position toward both you and your spouse. It may also cause your child to curtail a further sharing of feelings with you.

- **When the home situation is excessively disruptive or verbally abusive and your children go off to be alone, seek them out and comfort them.**

During family drinking episodes many children hide in the bathroom or their room because of fear or frustration. These episodes can be very upsetting. You should try to avoid letting your children go to sleep under upset conditions. If this occurs, talk with them at the first opportunity.

- **Avoid placing your oldest child in the position of being a confidant or surrogate parent to replace your spouse as parent.**

Making a surrogate parent of your child places too much strain on him or her and may also anger your spouse whose position your child is attempting to fulfill. Also, when the parent whose place they are taking resumes his or her duties, the child must revert to his or her original position in the family. This shifting of roles can lead your child to have feelings of inconsistency and to experience a serious personal problem.

- **Encourage and support your children to become involved in school and community activities.**

Your children, as others, need outlets and chances to develop needed relationships with others in activities outside of your home. Outside the home activities may help your child develop understandings that he or she can accomplish many things, and be independent of undesirable influences in your home.

- **Try to arrange times for your children to have their friends visit regularly.**

Your home should also be their home. Some alcoholics drink in patterns and provide some opportunity for normal family conditions. However, if your child has friends over and the alcoholic spouse is drinking, do not further embarrass your child or friends by confronting the alcoholic. The time to talk with an alcoholic about drinking is not when the drinking is taking place.

- **Avoid exacting promises from your children that they will never drink.**

If children of alcoholics decide to drink later in life, this promise may cause unneeded guilt. It will also imply to your child that he or she cannot handle alcohol. Many alcoholics have high levels of guilt about their drinking. Guilt may even increase their level of drinking because of their perceived inability, often learned in the home, to control alcohol consumption.

- **Avoid constantly asking your children if you should leave your spouse.**

Unless a separation has been decided upon, in which case the children should be consulted, questioning your children about when or if you should leave your spouse only adds to the children's confusion of why you remain together. This question is particularly inappropriate for small children. They feel that parents are supposed to be responsible and here a young child is being asked by a parent the most difficult of questions. Also, should a separation not occur, once you have raised these questions, your children may live in fear that a separation will occur at any time. This adds to your marital difficulties and to the personal problems of your children.

- **Educate yourself about alcoholism and community resources.**

It is difficult to help yourself or others unless you know what you are trying to work with. Much family frustration in alcoholic families arises from fears of unknown effects of drinking. Although you may not be able to get your spouse to stop drinking or to stop your own drinking, you can better prepare yourself and your children for survival.

- **Become involved in community resources or self-help groups for family members of alcoholics.**

Organizations such as Al-Anon and Alateen will greatly benefit the family. These groups provide for interaction and comradery with people in similar situations. Families of alcoholics need not be alone unless they choose to be.

- **If your alcoholic spouse seeks help, try to become involved as a family in the treatment process.**

Alcoholism affects the entire family and all will benefit from help. To allow the alcoholic to enter treatment alone is to deny a support structure for sobriety. Family members learn to adapt to the recovering alcoholic. Once the alcoholic quits drinking, family life will change. The family — which includes, of course, your child — must be prepared to accept the alcoholic member back into the family physically and emotionally. Total recovery from alcoholism may require a total family effort.

● **Do not dwell on the past, learn from it.**

Whether or not sobriety occurs, do not allow yourself to fall into the "what I could have done" syndrome. What you can do now is more important for your children. Their past is not as long as their future. Help your children by not making yesterday "eternal." To do so will always not only affect tomorrow, but will affect tomorrow negatively.

● **Use alternatives and new endeavors — not old habits.**

If the lives of you and your children are to get better change will be needed. This means alternatives and the investing of energy by you and your children to improve your lives. This will be difficult because of the usual lack of energy in the alcoholic home, but the family will not get better repeating negative behavior nor will it get better by doing nothing. Active alternatives are needed.

● **Stop doing what you do *not* do.**

Break your negative habits. For example, you do not discuss alcoholism, you do not get help, you do not try alternatives, you do not feel that anything will help, etc.. These habits become built in prohibitors or excuses to avoid recovery. You can stop negative inactivity by using positive actions.

● **Take care of yourself.**

It will be easier and far more realistic for you to help your children if you feel better about yourself. Your children need physically and emotionally healthy parents.

● **Get help! NOW!**

Do not wait for the right time. It has arrived. Many people feel that they will do something about the family situation when the time is right. Right for what? Postponing help only allows the problems to continue. Your children need you to act now. If you are concerned about protecting and helping your children, get help for them now. Do not deny their needs because you are not sure of yours.

At best implementation of these suggestions will provide some solutions for the problems within an alcoholic family. Only sobriety and family growth can overcome all the problems of alcoholism in the family.

Remember, if your children are to grow to have healthy and satisfying lives of their own, they need not only the help of people and friends in their community but most of all they will need you and the shared feelings, concern and love within a healthy family environment.

APPENDIX A

RESOURCE MATERIALS

Suggested Books and Articles

Al-Anon Family Group Headquarters, Inc. *Alateen: Hope for Children of Alcoholics,* revised edition; Al-Anon, 1980.

Barnard, Charles P. Families, *Alcoholism and Therapy.* Illinois: Thomas Books, 1981.

Black, Claudia. *It Will Never Happen To Me!* Denver, Colorado: Medical Administration Company , 1982.

Black, Claudia, *My Dad Loves Me, My Dad has a Disease.* Denver, Colorado: Medical Administration Company, 1982.

Brooks, Cathleen. *The Secret Everyone Knows.* San Diego, California: The Kroc Foundation, 1981.

Carroll, Charles R. *Alcohol: Use, Nonuse, and Abuse.* Dubuque, Iowa: Wm. C. Brown, 1975.

Chase, N.F. *A Child is Being Beaten: Violence Against Children; An American Tragedy.* New York: Holt, Rinehart & Winston, 1975.

Cohen, Sidney. *The Substance Abuse Problem.* New York: The Haworth Press, 1981.

Cork, Margaret R. *The Forgotten Children.* Ontario: Addiction Research Foundation, 1969.

Coudert, Jo. *The Alcoholic in Your Life.* New York: Stein & Day, 1981.

Deutsch, Charles. *Broken Bottles, Broken Dreams: Understanding and Helping the Children of Alcoholics.* New York: The Teachers College, 1982.

Erickson, Edsel; McEvoy, Alan and Colucci, Nicholas. *Child Abuse and Neglect: A Guidebook for Educators and Community Leaders.* Holmes Beach, Florida: Learning Publications, Inc. 1979.

Faber, Adele and Mazlish, Elaine. *Liberated Parents, Liberated Children.* New York: Avon Books, 1975.

Forrest, Gary G. *Confrontation in Psychotherapy with the Alcoholic.* Holmes Beach, Florida: Learning Publications, Inc., 1982.

Forrest, Gary G. *How to Live with a Problem Drinker and Survive.* New York: Antheneum, 1980.

Fox, Ruth. *The Effect of Alcoholism on Children.* National Council of Alcoholism, 1972.

Galanter, M., *Currents in Alcoholism: Volume VII.* New York: Grune & Stratton, 1980.

Ginnott, Haim. *Between Parent and Child.* New York: Avon Books, 1973.

Goodwin, Donald. *Is Alcoholism Hereditary?* New York: Oxford University Press, 1978.

Gordon, Thomas. *P.E.T. (Parent Effectiveness Training).* New York: Plume Books, New American Library, 1975.

Greenleaf, Jael. *Co-Alcoholic, Para-Alcoholic.* Los Angeles, California: Jael Greenleaf, 1981.

Hansen, Philip L. *Alcoholism: The Afflicted and the Affected.* Lake Mills, Iowa: Graphic Publishing Co., 1974.

Harwin, Judith and Orford, Jim. *Alcohol and the Family.* England: Croon Helm, 1980.

Hornik, Edith L. *You and Your Alcoholic Parent.* Associated Press, 1974.

Johnson, Vernon E. *I'll Quit Tomorrow.* New York: Harper & Row, 1980.

Kaufman, Edward and Kaufmann, Pauline. *Family Therapy of Drug and Alcohol Abuse.* New York: Gardener Press, Inc., 1979.

Keller, John E. *Alcohol. A Family Affair. Help for Families in Which There is Alcohol Misuse.* Santa Ynez, California: The Kroc Foundation, 1977.

Kempe, Henry C. and Kempe, Ruth. *Child Abuse.* Denver, Colorado: Kempe Publishing Co., 1978.

Kempe, Henry and Helfer, Ray E. *The Battered Child,* Third Edition, Denver, Colorado: Kempe Publishing Co., 1980.

Kempe, Henry C. and Helfer, Ray E. *Helping the Battered Child and His Family.* New York: Harper and Row, 1972.

Knox, Laura. *Parents are People, Too.* Englewood Cliffs, New Jersey: Prentice-Hall, 1980.

Leach, Penelope. *Babyhood.* New York: Alfred A. Knopf, Inc.

Leboyer, Frederick. *Birth Without Violence.* New York: Alfred A. Knopf, Inc., 1975.

Leshan, Eda. *What Makes Me Feel This Way?* New York: Macmillan, Inc., 1972.

Mahoney, Barbara. *A Sensitive, Passionate Man.* New York: Pyramid, Inc., 1975.

Martin, Joseph C. *No Laughing Matter: Chalk Talks About Alcohol.* New York: Harper and Row, 1982.

Maxwell, Ruth. *The Booze Battle.* New York: Ballantine Books, 1976.

Mayer, Adele. *Incest: A Treatment Manual for Therapy with Victims, Spouses, and Offenders.* Holmes Beach, Florida: Learning Publications, Inc., 1983.

McAfee, O. and Nedler, S. *Education for Parenthood: A Primary Prevention Strategy for Child Abuse and Neglect.* (Report No. 93), Denver, Colorado: Education Commission of the States, 1976.

McCabe, Thomas R. *Victims No More.* Center City, Minnesota: Hazelden, 1978.

Milgram, G. G. *Alcohol Education Materials: An Annotated Bibliography.* New Jersey: Rutgers University Press, 1981.

Minuchin, Salvadore. *Families and Family Therapy.* Cambridge, Massachusetts: Harvard University Press, 1976.

Rebeta-Burditt, Joyce. *The Cracker Factory.* New York: Macmillan, Inc., 1977.

Research Monograph #4, *Services for Children of Alcoholics.* Symposium, Silver Springs, Maryland, 1979. DHHS publication #ADM 81-1007.

Scott, Edward M. *Struggles in an Alcoholic Family.* Springfield, Illinois: Charles Thomas Book, 1970.

Seixas, Judith S. *Living with a Parent who Drinks Too Much.* New York: Greenwillow Books, Div. of Wm. Morrow and Co., 1979.

Shouse, Dennis; Blevins, Gregory and Simpson, Dennis. *Handbook for Volunteers in Substance Abuse Agencies.* Holmes Beach, Florida: Learning Publications, Inc., 1983.

Snyder, Anne. *First Step.* New York: Holt, Rinehart and Winston, 1975.

Spock, Benjamin, M.D. *Baby and Child Care.* New York: Pocket Books, 1981.

Steiner, Claude. *Games Alcoholics Play.* New York: Ballantine Books, Inc., 1977.

Stimmel, Barry. *The Effects of Maternal Alcohol and Drug Abuse on the Newborn.* New York: Hawthorne Press, 1983.

Twerski, Abraham J. *Caution: Kindness can be Dangerous to the Alcoholic.* Englewood Cliffs, New Jersey: Prentice-Hall, Inc., 1981.

Wegscheider, Sharon. *A Second Chance.* Palo Alto, California: Science and Behavior Books, 1980.

Woititz, Janet Geringer. *Marriage on the Rocks; Learning to Live with Yourself and an Alcoholic.* New York: Delacorte Press, 1979.

Young, Leontine. *Life Among the Giants.* New York: McGraw-Hill, Inc., 1966.

Suggested Pamphlets

Many agencies produce helpful materials for the alcoholic family. A list of such pamphlets is listed below according to source.

Al-Anon/Alateen Family Group Headquarters, Inc.
P.O. Box 182
Madison Square Station
New York, New York 10010

Adult Children of Alcoholics. Al-Anon, 1979.

If Your Parents Drink Too Much. Al-Anon, 1974.

Living with an Alcoholic: With the Help of Al-Anon. Al-Anon, 1980.

Addiction Research Foundation Dept.
c/o Marketing Services
33 Russell Street
Toronto, Ontario, Canada M552S1

Alcoholism And The Family
In this easily read, illustrated pamphlet, Dr. Meeks, Director of the School for Addiction Studies at the Research Foundation, suggests ways in which families can confront the problem drinker and seek the necessary help that they will need to support the recovering alcoholic.

Alcoholism—A Merry-Go-Round Named Denial
This publication describes the development process of a problem drinker into a full-fledged alcoholic. In the form of a three-part play, it explains how the wife, friends, and employer may, in fact, contribute to the problem. Alternatives are suggested to short circuit this development process. (12 pages)

Alcoholics Anonymous World Services, Inc.
P.O. Box 459, Grand Central Station
New York, New York 10163
(212) 686-1100

Is There An Alcoholic In Your Life?
Explains the A.A. program as it affects anyone close to an alcoholic—spouse, other family members, friends.

44 Questions
Answers the questions most frequently asked about A.A. by alcoholics seeking help as well as by their families and friends.

The American Humane Association
P.O. Box 1266
Denver, Colorado 80201

Discipline, Your Child And You
by Robert Blum & Lynne Blum
Contains helpful insights on a subject about which most parents hold strong feelings and expectations. For parents and for those who help, this publication offers an important up-to-date perspective on discipline and how children grow and learn. (16 pages)

Emotional Neglect of Children by Robert M. Mulford
A penetrating analysis of the challenge to child protection posed by this difficult area of child neglect. (11 pages)

Guidelines For Schools:
Teachers, Nurses, Counselors and Administrators
This pamphlet provides a brief but useful review of the child abuse and neglect problem with an emphasis on how school personnel can assist in the resolution of the problem. A list of "indicators" is identified dealing with both the child's behavior and appearance as well as typical parental attitudes which might suggest abusive or negligent treatment.

A National Symposium On Child Abuse
An interdisciplinary exploration of child abuse and sexual exploitation of children. Papers given at a national symposium which examined the intensity of the problem and discussed the legal, medical, and protective aspects of the problem. (72 pages)

Neglecting Parents by Morron Cohen, Robert Mulford, and Elizabeth Philbrick
Interpretation of the findings in a research project to identify the psychosocial characteristics of neglecting parents in almost 1,000 families. (28 pages)

Protecting The Battered Child by Edgar Menll, Irving Kaufman, Philip Dodge and Arthur Schoepfer
Report of a statewide study and analysis of child abuse cases; discussion of implications as viewed by experts in psychiatry, medicine, law and social work. (30 pages)

Termination Of Parental Rights by Vincent De Francis
Explores the problem of termination of parental rights and the legal complications which surround the process. Basic data with respect to the rights of parents and children, and variations on the theme of how parental rights are affected, presented and discussed. (20 pages)

Treating Parental Pathology by Elizabeth Philbrick
A superb exposition of how authority in casework is employed in the process of treating the pathology of neglecting parents. (18 pages)

Working With Parents And Children In Day Care
by Thelma Baily and Pearl Kerr
This is a practical guide to those involved in child care or who work with children in some way. Children's feelings, perceptions, experiences and behaviors are considered with specific suggestions for child management techniques. (23 pages)

CASPAR Alcohol Education Program
226 Highland Avenue
Somerville, MA 02143

Decisions About Drinking (Grades 3-12)
by Dixie Mills, Charles Deutsch, Lena DiCicco, 1978

Comprehensive Health Education Foundation
20814 Pacific Highway South
Seattle, WA 98188

Here's Looking At You by Clay Roberts

Education Commission of the States
300 Lincoln Tower, 1860 Lincoln Street
Denver, Colorado 80203

Child Abuse and Neglect: Model Legislation For The States (Report No. 71)
This pamphlet contains an examination of how legislation can improve state and local efforts to combat child abuse and neglect. It encourages state legislators to review their existing laws and revise them where appropriate. Model legislation is suggested and is accompanied by a text explaining why certain provisions are included.

Education For Parenthood: A Primary Prevention Strategy For Child Abuse And Neglect (Report No. 93)
This pamphlet examines parenting education as a potentially useful strategy in combating child abuse and neglect. A rationale for parent education is included along with a suggested plan of action aimed at initiating curriculum development in this area of study.

Education Policies And Practices Regarding Child Abuse
And Neglect, And Recommendations For Policy
Development (Report No. 85)
This pamphlet reports on the findings of a survey aimed at
assessing the frequency of policy development at state and
local levels in the area of child abuse and neglect. A suggested policy statement with detailed explanation of each
of its components is included.

National Center on Child Abuse and Neglect
P.O. Box 1182
Washington, D.C. 20013

Careers In Child Abuse And Neglect:
Many Ways To Help, 1981
Describes careers and professions that provide help for victims of child abuse and neglect. The pamphlet features a
bibliography of films and books, together with the names
and addresses of professional organizations involved in the
child abuse and neglect field. (20 pages)

Daniel El Travieso:
Como Manejar La Tension Familiar, 1981
This Spanish-language, "comic-book" style booklet uses
the characters of "Dennis the Menace" cartoon strip to
show how stress can affect relationships between parents
and their children, and suggests ways to deal with such
pressures. (16 pages)

Families In Stress, 1979
This is intended for parents facing pressures that might
lead to abusive behavior. It discusses stress that parents
face and how and where they can obtain relief. (24 pages)

Family Violence: Intervention Strategies by R. B. Barnett, C. B. Pittman, C. K. Ragan, M. K. Salus, 1980
The nature, extent and possible treatment of domestic violence are examined with special attention given to the role of the child protective services workers in assisting violent families. (81 pages)

National Study Of The Incidence And Severity Of Child Abuse And Neglect: Executive Summary, 1981
Summarizes the findings of analyzed data collected between May 1979 and April 1980. Topics discussed include the number of reported and estimated cases, the incidence rate and numbers of the major forms of child maltreatment, and age and sex of the children involved. (17 pages)

Parenting: An Annotated Bibliography, 1981
Contains descriptions and bibliographic information for several dozen books on various aspects of parenting and parent education. Specific topics covered include parenting for teenagers and single parents, working mothers, discipline, and behavior modification. (34 pages)

Profile On Neglect: A Survey Of The State Of Knowledge Of Child Neglect, 1976
Examines various aspects of child neglect, including legal, professional, and operational definitions of neglect, its causes, identification, and treatment. A bibliography of approximately 100 articles and other documents on neglect is included. (57 pages)

Selected Readings On Adolescent Maltreatment, 1981
Included are eleven papers on various aspects of the maltreatment of adolescents. Topics covered include the incidence of teenage abuse and neglect, sexually mistreated
adolescents, intervention and service delivery, and the
physical abuse of adolescents. (115 pages)

National Committee for Prevention of Child Abuse
Suite 510
111 East Wacker Drive
Chicago, IL 60601

A Look At Child Abuse
This pamphlet is written in laymen's language and is helpful for teachers, volunteers, physicians, troubled parents
and students who want to become acquainted with the
problem. Its chapters include: "What is Abuse," "Childhood's Seamy Past," "Looking for Causes," "Child Abuse
and the Law," "Ways to Stop Child Abuse," and "Blueprint
for Action."

Public Affairs Pamphlets
381 Park Avenue South
New York, New York 10016

You And Your Alcoholic Parent by Edith Lynn Hornik

Rutgers Center of Alcohol Studies
Publications Division
New Brunswick, NJ 08903

Adjustment Of The Family To The Crisis of Alcoholism
by Joan K. Jackson

Alcohol-Related Acts Of Violence: Who Was Drinking And Where The Acts Occurred by L. W. Gerson

The Alcoholic's Spouse, Children, And Family Interactions: Substantive Findings And Methodological Issues by T. Jacob, A. Favorini, S. S. Meisel and C. M. Anderson

Alcoholism And Child Abuse: A Review by T. C. Orme and J. Rimmer

Children Of Alcoholics, Report Of A Preliminary Study And Comments On The Literature by C. Wilson and J. Orford

Disrupted Family Rituals: A Factor In The Intergenerational Transmission Of Alcoholism by S. J. Wolin, L. A. Bennett, D. L. Noonan, and M. A. Teitelbaum

The Effects Of Drinking On Offspring: A Historical Survey Of The American And British Literature by R. H. Warner and H. L. Rosett

Family Therapy With The Families Of Recovering Alcoholics by D. E. Meeks and C. Kelly

Suggested Films

ACI Media
Division of Paramount Oxford Films
35 W. 45th Street
New York, New York 10036
(212) 582-6100

> *Child Molesters: Fact and Fiction*
> (sexual abuse) (30 minutes), 1976.
> Documenting information about molesters, the film analyzes pedophilia, showing examples from typical cases. A group discusses myths contrasted to facts about child molesters.

A.C.T.
P.O. Box 8536
Newport Beach, California 92660
(714) 499-4806

> *Children of Denial* (28 minutes).
> Film about youngsters, adolescents, and adults as children of alcoholics. Three basic tenants rule the lives of these children—Don't TALK—Don't TRUST—Don't FEEL.

Addition Research Foundation
33 Russell Street
Toronto, Ontario
Canada M55 251
(416) 595-6056

> *Children of Alcoholics* (15 minutes), 1980.
> A look at treatment programs for the children of alcoholics
> in California documenting the effects of alcoholism on
> both juveniles and adults who have parents that drink too
> much.

AIMS Media Inc.
626 Hustin Avenue
Glendale, California 91201
(213) 240-9300

> *All Bottled Up* (29 minutes), 1975.
> Highlights of child's perspective of alcoholic parents.

> *Counseling the Children of Alcoholics*
> by Kathleen Michael (21 minutes), 1979.
> In their concern for the alcoholic, counselors often have
> overlooked other members of the family — particularly
> children. In this tape, she vividly details her technique for
> dealing with these "forgotten children." She explains how
> to set up a counseling program for the children of alco-
> holics and identifies the essential qualities of a good
> counselor.

That's Marilyn (28 minutes), 1980.
This is a dramatic program about the children of alcoholics and provides an understanding of some of the
sufferings of thousands of young people in our communities. Designed for teenage and adult audiences, this video-
tape will spark a sympathetic discussion on these issues.

Audio Visual Services
Special Service Building
The Pennsylvania State University
University Park, Pennsylvania 16802
(814) 865-6314

Child Abuse: Cradle of Violence (20 minutes), 1976.
Intimate interviews with abusive parents in the area of
child behavior and discipline create an understanding of
child abuse and the need to break the cycle. Alternatives
to corporal punishment and potential stress situations are
presented.

What About Tomorrow?, 1975.
Young adolescents who experiment with alcohol are the
subject of this film. It follows a group through a party
where alcohol is present and one boy loses control of his
drinking and finds himself face-to-face with the town
inebriate he and his friend were teasing earlier that day.

Brigham Young University
Media Marketing W-STAD
Provo, Utah 84602
(801) 374-1211 Ext. 4071

Cipher in the Snow (emotional abuse) (24 minutes), 1973. An Award-winning film, this dramatization of psychological abuse is based on the true story of a boy no one thought was important until his sudden death one snowy morning.

Do As I Do (29 minutes), 1974.
Parent's role in prevention of alcohol abuse. Views of how children copy their parent's actions and attitudes.

Fetal Alcohol Syndrome (13 minutes), 1975.
Over one-half of the babies born to alcoholic mothers are retarded, victims of permanent fetal damage. Symptoms of this form of retardation at birth; development of the children.

The Secret Love of Sandra Blain (28 minutes), 1970.
Step-by-step dramatization of the progression into alcoholism of a wife and mother, showing how her unrecognized illness affects her family, friends, physician, and herself.

Department of Audio-Visual Communications
Brigham Young University
Provo, Utah 84601

Bitter Wind (30 minutes).
The story of a Navajo family and the attempts of a son to reunite his alcoholic family.

Consortium C
1750 Seamist Box 863
Houston, Texas 77008

Lift a Finger: The Teacher's Role in Combating Child Abuse and Neglect, 1976.

This is a three part presentation of the child abuse and neglect problem which consists of four (4) slide trays and three (3) accompanying tapes. Prepared for use by school personnel in the state of Texas, it nevertheless offers a useful analysis of the problem and a suggested range of strategies helpful to professionals in other states. The program covers three topics: (1) An overview of child abuse; (2) Identification and referral; and (3) Legal aspects. A detailed study guide, including evaluation instruments, accompanies the program. Persons offering in-service workshops for teachers and school staff will find it a helpful resource.

Father Martin Associates, Inc.
8 Howard Street
Aberdeen, Maryland 21001-2494
(301) 272-1975

Chalk Talk (1 hour).
A discussion of alcohol and the body as well as various views on alcoholism.

The 12 Steps of AA (45 minutes), 1981.
In a lecture setting, Father Martin provides comments on the meaning of each of the 12 steps. He then demonstrates the natural progression from the first step to the last, and shows how together the steps provide a framework for recovery from alcoholism.

FMS Productions, Inc.
1777 North Vine Street
Los Angeles, California 90028
(213) 461-4567

> *Alcoholism and the Family* (42 minutes), 1977.
> This program points out the effect of alcoholism on the family before and after sobriety.

> *Guidelines* (45 minutes).
> Attitudes and values about alcohol and alcoholism are examined. Practical guidelines to help the alcoholic are explored.

> *Intervention and Recovery* (30 minutes), 1982.
> This film is intended to introduce the concept of intervention to family, friends, and employers who want to help the alcohol-or-drug-addict person.

Focal Point
Box 207
Pomfret, Connecticut 06258
(203) 974-0159

> *Alcohol and Alcoholism: I and II, Portrait of an Alcoholic* (45 minutes), 1981.
> The images many people have about alcoholic persons are contrasted with the facts about the illness of alcoholism. Alternatives left to those alcoholics who continue to drink are shown and compared to options for treatment for those who strive to recover from alcoholism.

Alcohol Awareness (52 minutes), 1981.
This filmstrip series is intended to provide students in grades 5-8 with information on alcohol to stimulate responsible decisions about drinking. The four filmstrips in the series are: (1) About Alcohol (2) How Alcohol Affects the Body (3) Why Drink? Why Abstain? (4) Using and Misusing Alcohol.

Health Sciences Consortium
200 Eastowne Drive
Suite 213
Chapel Hill, North Carolina 27514
(919) 942-8731

Alcoholism, A Family Problem (13 minutes), 1978.
A dramatization of three stages of alcoholism as it affects family members. Explores the feelings and behaviors typical of each stage.

Indiana University
Audio-Visual Center
Bloomington, Indiana 47401
(812) 337-8087

The Battered Child (58 minutes), 1969.
This is a documentary study of child abuse based on the book *The Battered Child* by Drs. C. Henry Kempe and Ray E. Hefler.

Johnson Institute
10700 Olson Memorial Highway
Minneapolis, Minnesota 55441
(612) 544-4165

A Story About Feelings (10 minutes), 1981.
Produced for children ages 5 through 8. Uses both live and animated scenes to present the story of a young boy named John, who begins to smoke to feel cool. As kids tell the story, the film graphically shows the deterioration of John's adult behavior and his relationships. The message of illness as opposed to badness is emphasized as John is taken to the hospital because he took more pills and drinks than his body could handle.

Learning Corporation of America
1350 Avenue of the Americas
New York, New York 10019
(212) 397-9360

She Drinks a Little (31 minutes), 1981.
Teenager Cindy Stott has an alcoholic mother whose drinking is destroying both of their lives. With the help of a male classmate with a similar problem, Cindy discovers Alateen and learns how to deal with her mother.

Learning Publications, Inc.
Box 1326, Dept. COA-100
Holmes Beach, Florida 33509

Children of Alcoholics (38 minutes), 1982.
Designed for use with therapists, counselors, and other professionals. This video cassette discusses the special treatment needs for working with children of alcoholics and their families.

Mr. James Martin
High Court of Southern California
100 Border Avenue
Solana Beach, California 92075
(714) 755-5158

> *Fragile—Handle with Care* (overview of child abuse and neglect) (26 minutes), 1975.
> Narrated by Bill Cosby, the film shows that abuse of children is an old but increasing problem and examines why parents abuse their children and what happens to the children, both physically and mentally. The film looks at ways of preventing child abuse and deals with the legal considerations involved. The situations portrayed are reenactments of authentic case histories.

Maryland Center for Public Broadcasting
11767 Bonita Avenue
Owings Mills, Maryland 21117
(301) 356-5600

> *Soft is the Heart of a Child* (30 minutes), 1980.
> Depicts through drama the effects of alcoholism on the family, especially the children.

McGraw-Hill Films
330 West 42nd Street
New York, New York 10036

> *The Summer We Moved to Elm Street* (30 minutes), 1968.
> The family of an alcoholic is depicted through the eyes of a nine-year-old girl.

Media Guild
118 South Acacia
Box 887
Solana, California 92075
(714) 755-9191

> *Raised in Anger* (58 minutes).
> Reveals why so many otherwise ordinary parents are abusing their children and describes effective prevention programs to deal with this problem.

Media Services
Child Development and Mental Health Center
University of Washington
Seattle, Washington 98795
(206) 543-4011

> *Right From the Start* (9 minutes), 1980.
> Aimed at pregnant social drinkers, this public education slide-tape presentation discusses a healthy pregnancy from a newborn infant's point of view. Nutrition and exercise are stressed, and the harmful effects of alcohol are explained.

In Arkansas, Kansas, Louisiana, Missouri, Oklahoma and Texas, contact:
Motorola Teleprograms, Inc.
7919 Cliffbrook Drive
Suite 243
Dallas, Texas 75240
(214) 661-8464 call collect

In Alaska, Hawaii and Illinois, contact:
Motorola Teleprograms, Inc.
4825 North Scott Street
Suite 23
Schiller Park, Illinois 60176
(312) 671-0141 call collect

In all other states, contact: The Illinois address, or call
toll-free (800) 323-1900

> *Don't Give Up on Me* (social workers) (28 minutes), 1975.
> Accompanied by an instructor's manual and useful for
> social workers, the film's emphasis is on understanding and
> helping parents so overwhelmed by problems that they lash
> out at their youngsters. Only one character in the case, a
> social worker, is played by a professional actor. Therapists,
> counselors, abusive parents and their children play them-
> selves.

> *The Last Taboo* (sexual abuse) (30 minutes), 1977.
> Intended for public information, this film explains sexual
> abuse of children, including the effects on and the feelings
> of the victim.

MTI Teleprograms, Inc.
37110 Commercial Avenue
Northbrook, Illinois 60062
(312) 291-5343

> *Interviewing the Abused Child* (22 minutes), 1978.
> Children of various ages, subjected to different types of
> abuse, are seen and heard as professionals talk with them.
> Invites viewers to form their own judgments about the
> effectiveness of four different types of interview techniques.

New Day Films
P.O. Box 315
Franklin Lakes, New Jersey 07417
(212) 581-3280

> *The Last to Know* (55 minutes), 1981.
> In this film, four women from different socioeconomic, racial and ethic backgrounds comment about their involvement with alcohol and prescribed drugs. They describe how alcoholism affects all aspects of their lives, from work to sexual involvement, to their fundamental self-image and the experiences of being an addict. In addition the responsibility of the pharmaceutical and alcoholic beverage industries in promoting the use of alcohol and drugs by women.

Onsite Training & Consulting, Inc.
P.O. Box 3790
Minneapolis, Minnesota 55403

> *Another Change* (30 minutes).
> The story line is based on Mary Lee, from a dependent home, who grew up in a tense atmosphere of fear, guilt, etc. Sharon guides Mary Lee in an exploration of her feelings relating to situations not only from her own past but also of other family members.

> *Family Aftercare and Recovery* (30 minutes).
> People going home after treatment want things to be different without change. In this presentation, Wegscheider explains why and how to a group of people preparing to go back to their families. She outlines the requirements for care after treatment and full recovery for the family in every aspect.

The Family Trap (30 minutes).
Offers the first complete picture of the pressures which contribute to the family illness, and the hope and help there is for family members to achieve recovery through intervention, identification and counseling.

Sculpturing (30 minutes).
Wegscheider uses sculpturing, a technique in which family members are physically placed in positions symbolizing their feelings—a vivid demonstration showing how chemical dependency fragments and destroys the unity of the family system.

Operation Cork
8939 Villa La Folla Drive
San Diego, California 92037
(714) 452-5716

If You Loved Me (54 minutes).
Chronicles the almost-classic deterioration of a family because of alcoholism. The arguing, the tears, the frustrations, and the denial. Finally the wife accepts a friend's advice to go to a meeting of Al-Anon.

RMI Media Productions
120 West 72nd Street
Kansas City, Missouri 64114

Family Arena (15 minutes), 1977.
This cartoon filmstrip parodies the family conflicts caused by alcoholism or other chemical dependency in a family member. It also shows that in a chemically dependent family, denial is the chief symptom and family roles are interrelated. Offers a quiz to see if chemical dependency exists in a family, and identifies sources of help.

University of Connecticut
Media and the Arts for Social Services
U-Box 127
Storrs, Connecticut 06268
(203) 486-4888

The Game (28 minutes), 1977.
This film focuses on two families (one affluent, one blue collar) who are having difficulties with alcohol. The affluent alcoholic is an active drinker who realizes he needs help with his drinking problem, while the blue collar man is a recovering alcoholic who finds returning to his family a rewarding experience.

Suffer the Children (37 minutes), 1978.
Follows three case workers who are responding to suspected child abuse or neglect calls.

WHA-TV Distribution Department
821 University Avenue
Madison, Wisconsin 53706
(608) 263-2121

One for My Baby (27 minutes), 1982.
Presents information about fetal alcohol syndrome (FAS).
Discussed are the symptoms of FAS as well as the relative
risks to the unborn when women drink during pregnancy.
Two couples who have FAS children—one natural-born,
one adopted—are interviewed, and describe their feelings
about the syndrome as the camera focuses on the children.

Xerox Films
Xerox Educational Publications
245 Long Hill Road
Middletown, Connecticut 06457
(203) 347-7251

Children in Peril (physical abuse and neglect) (22 minutes),
1975.
This film reports that, according to medical authorities,
the leading cause of infant death in the United States may
well be murder at the hands of the infant's own parents.
According to the film, there were some 60,000 reported
cases of child abuse in the United States in 1974, and an
estimated two children die of abuse each day in this country alone. The film also reveals that child abusers are not
strikingly different from nonabusive adults.

APPENDIX B

RESOURCE AGENCIES

Resource Agencies

Addiction Research Foundation
33 Russell Street
Toronto, Ontario, Canada M5S251

Al-Anon/Alateen Family Group Headquarters, Inc.
P.O. Box 182
Madison Square Station
New York, New York 10010

Alcoholics Anonymous World Services, Inc.
468 Park Avenue South
New York, New York 10016

American Humane Association
Children's Division
P.O. Box 1266
Denver, Colorado 80201

Child Care Information Center
532 Settlers Landing Road
P.O. Box 548
Hampton, Virginia 23669

Child Welfare League of America, Inc.
67 Irving Place
New York, New York 10003

Children Are People, Inc.
1599 Selby Ave.
St. Paul, Minnesota 55104

Community Intervention, Inc.
220 South Tenth St.
Minneapolis, Minnesota 55403

Do It Now Foundation
National Media Center
P.O. Box 5115
Phoenix, Arizona 85010

Drug Abuse Council
1828 L. Street, NW
Washington, D.C. 20036

Drug Enforcement Administration
1405 Eye Street, NW
Washington, DC 20537

MultiCultural Resource Center
8443 Crenshaw Boulevard
Inglewood, California 90305

National Association for Children of Alcoholics
P.O. Box 421691
San Francisco, California 94142

National Center for Alcohol Education
1901 North Moore Street
Arlington, Virginia 22209

National Center on Child Abuse and Neglect
United States Children's Bureau
Office of Child Development, DHEW
Washington, D.C. 20013

Region I: Connecticut, Maine, Massachusetts, New
              Hampshire, Rhode Island, Vermont

              Child Abuse and Neglect Resource Center
              New England Resource Center
              295 Longwood Avenue
              Boston, Massachusetts 02115
              (617) 232-8390

Region II: New Jersey, New York, Puerto Rico, Virgin
              Islands

              Child Abuse and Neglect Resource Center
              College of Human Ecology
              Family Life Development Center
              E-200, MVR Hall
              Cornell University
              Ithaca, New York 14853
              (607) 256-7794

Region III: Delaware, District of Columbia, Maryland,
              Pennsylvania, Virginia, West Virginia

              Child Abuse and Neglect Resource Center
              Institute for Urban Affairs and Research
              Howard University
              2900 Van Ness St., NW
              Washington, D.C. 20008
              (202) 686-6770

Region IV: Alabama, Florida, Georgia, Kentucky,
              Mississippi, North Carolina, Tennessee

              Child Abuse and Neglect Resource Center
              Regional Institute of Social Welfare
              Research, Inc.
              P.O. Box 152
              455 N. Milledge Ave.
              Athens, Georgia 30603
              (403) 542-7614

Region V: Illinois, Indiana, Michigan, Minnesota,
              Ohio, Wisconsin

              Child Abuse and Neglect Resource Center
              Center for Advanced Studies in Human Services
              School of Social Welfare
              University of Wisconsin-Milwaukee
              P.O. Box 786
              Milwaukee, Wisconsin 53201
              (414) 963-4184

Region VI: Arkansas, Louisiana, New Mexico, Texas,
              Oklahoma

              Child Abuse and Neglect Resource Center
              University of Texas at Austin
              2609 University Avenue
              Austin, Texas 78712
              (512) 471-4067

Region VII: Iowa, Kansas, Missouri, Nebraska

Child Abuse and Neglect Resource Center
Institute of Child Behavior and Development
University of Iowa-Oakdale Campus
Oakdale, Iowa 52319
(319) 353-4791

Region VIII: Colorado, Montana, North Dakota, South
Dakota, Utah, Wyoming

Child Abuse and Neglect Resource Center
1205 Oneida St.
Denver, Colorado 80220
(303) 321-3963

Region IX: Arizona, California, Hawaii, Nevada, Guam,
Pacific Trust Territories

Child Abuse and Neglect Resource Center
Department of Special Education
California State University-Los Angeles
5151 State University Drive
Los Angeles, California 90032
(213) 224-3283

Region X: Alaska, Idaho, Oregon, Washington

Child Abuse and Neglect Resource Center
157 Yesler Way, Suite 208
Seattle, Washington 98104
(206) 624-1062

National Center for the Prevention and Treatment of Child
   Abuse and Neglect
University of Colorado Medical Center
1205 Oneida Street
Denver, Colorado 80220

National Center for Voluntary Action
1785 Massachusetts Avenue, NW
Washington, D.C. 20036

National Clearinghouse for Alcohol Information
P.O. Box 2345
Rockville, Maryland 20850

National Clearinghouse for Drug Abuse Information
P.O. Box 1908
Rockville, Maryland 20850

National Coalition for Children's Justice
66 Witherspoon Street
Princeton, New Jersey 08540

National Committee for Prevention of Child Abuse
Suite 510
111 East Wacker Drive
Chicago, Illinois 60601

National Coordinating Council of Drug Education
1526 18th Street, NW
Washington, D.C. 20036

National Council on Alcoholism
2 Park Avenue
New York, New York 10016

National Institute on Alcohol Abuse and Alcoholism
5600 Fishers Lane
Rockville, Maryland 20857

National Institute of Drug Abuse
11400 Rockville Pike
Rockville, Maryland 20852

Operation Cork
8939 Villa La Jolla Drive
San Diego, California 92037
(714) 452-5716

Parental Stress Service, Inc.
154 Santa Clara Avenue
Oakland, California 95610

Parents Anonymous
National Office
2810 Artesia Boulevard
Redondo Beach, California 90278

Rutgers Center of Alcohol Studies
P.O. Box 969
Piscataway, New Jersey 08854

REFERENCES

Ackerman, R. J. "Socio-Cultural Aspects of Substance Abuse." *Competency-Based Training Manual for Substance Abuse Counselors,* Office of Substance Abuse Services, Department of Health, Michigan, 1978.

Ackerman, R. J. "Alcoholism and The Family." Paper presented at the University of Akron Conference on Alcoholism: The New Perspective, April 23, 1982

Alcohol Fact Sheet. New York: National Council on Alcoholism, 1976.

Berry, R. E. *The Economic Cost of Alcohol Abuse.* New York: Free Press, 1977.

Bosma, W. G. A. "Alcoholism and Teenagers." *Maryland State Medical Journal,* 1975.

Brookover, W., & Erickson, E. L. *Sociology of Education.* Illinois: Dorsey Press, 1975.

Brooks, C., *The Secret Everyone Knows,* California: Operation Cork, 1981.

Chafetz, M. E., Blane, H. T., & Hill, M. J. "Children of Alcoholism: Observations in a Child Guidance Clinic." *Quarterly Journal of Alcohol Studies,* 1971.

Coates, M. and Paech, Gail. *Alcohol and Your Patient: A Nurse's Handbook.* Canada: Addiction Research Foundation, 1979.

Cork, M. R. *The Forgotten Children,* Canada: Addictive Research Foundation, 1969.

Craig, G. H. *Human Development.* New Jersey: Prentice-Hall, Inc., 1976.

Deutch, Charles. *Broken Bottles Broken Dreams.* New York: Teachers College Press, 1982.

Erikson, E.H. *Childhood and Society.* New York: W. W. Norton and Co., 1963.

Fine, E., Yudin, L. W., Holmes, J., & Heinemann, S., "Behavior Disorders in Children with Parental Alcoholism." Paper presented at the Annual Meeting of the National Council on Alcoholism, Milwaukee, 1975.

Fontana, V. *Somewhere A Child is Crying.* New York: New American Library, 1976.

Forrest, G. G. *The Diagnosis and Treatment of Alcoholism.* New York: Charles C. Thomas, 1975.

Fox, R. "The Effect of Alcoholism on Children." New York: National Council on Alcoholism, 1972.

Garmezy, Norman et al. as reported by Eleanor Hoover in *Human Behavior,* April, 1976.

Hall, C.S., & Lindzey, G. *Theories of Personality.* New York: John Wiley & Sons, Inc., 1970.

Hecht, M. "A Cooperative Approach Towards Children from Alcoholic Families." *Elementary School Guidance and Counseling,* February, 1977.

Hindman, M. "Children of Alcoholic Parents." *Alcohol World Health & Research,* Rockville, Maryland: NIAAA, Winter, 1975-76.

Hornik, E. L. *You and Your Alcoholic Parent.* New York: Association Press, 1974.

Jackson, J. K. "The Adjustment of the Family to the Crises of Alcoholism." *Quarterly Journal of Studies on Alcohol,* 1954.

Jones, K. L., Smith, D. W., Ulleland, C., & Streissguth, A.P. "Patterns of Malformation in Offspring of Chronic Alcoholic Mothers." *Lancet,* 1973.

Lee E. E. "Alcohol Education and the Elementary School Teacher." *The Journal of School Health,* 1976.

McKay, J. R., et al. "Juvenile Delinquency and Drinking Behavior." *Journal of Health and Human Behavior,* 1963.

Milgram, G. G. "Current Status and Problems of Alcohol Education in the Schools." *The Journal of School Health,* 1976.

Morehouse, E., "Working in the Schools with Children of Alcoholic Parents." *Health and Social Work* Vol. 4, No. 4, 1979.

National Institute on Alcohol Abuse and Alcoholism. *Facts About Alcohol and Alcoholism,* Rockville, Maryland: NIAAA, 1980.

Nylander, I. "Children of Alcoholic Fathers." *Acta Paediatrica,* 1960.

Oswald, R. M. *The Development and Function of Personality.* Morristown, New Jersey: General Learning Press, 1976.

Papalia, D. E., & Olds, S. W. *Human Development.* McGraw-Hill, Inc., 1978.

Reddy, B., "Alcoholism, A Family Illness". Park Ridge, Illinois: Lutheran General Hospital.

Solomon, T. "History and Demography of Child Abuse." *Pediatrics,* 1973.

Wegscheider, Sharon. "Children of Alcoholics Caught in Family Trap." *Focus on Alcohol and Drug Issues 2,* May-June, 1979.

Weir, W. R. "Counseling Youth Whose Parents are Alcoholic: A Means to an End as Well as an End in Itself." *Journal of Alcohol Education,* 1970.

Westchester County Department of Community Mental Health, "Student Assistance Program Summary." 1981.

INDEX

Al-Anon, 113, 156
Alateen, 113-114, 156
Alcohol education, 81-85,
    116, 156
  child's behavior, 103
  course content, 87-89
  in-service training, 107-108
  objectives, 87
  teacher credibility, 85-86
Alcoholism
  degree, 6
Alcoholics, 3, 4
  behavior, 25-26
  female, 10, 54, 55, 61
  male, 10, 54, 61
  type, 7
Alcoholics Anonymous, 114
Child abuse
  emotional, 57
  physical, 57, 62-63, 98
Child development
  emotional, 63, 66
  personality, 67-76
  physical, 60-63

Childhood crises,
  trust vs. mistrust, 68
  autonomy vs. shame, 69
  initiative vs. guilt, 70
  industry vs. inferiority, 71
  identity vs. diffusion, 72
  intimacy vs. isolation, 73
  generativity vs. self
      absorption, 74
  integrity vs. disgust, 75
Children
  behavior, 27, 101-102
  feelings, 140
  roles, 44, 52, 53, 153-154
Childrens' perceptions, 7, 8, 49
  on brothers and sisters, 52
  on drinking, 55, 136, 155
  powerlessness, 55, 136-137
  self-concept, 66, 70, 110
Collective mind, 6
Community activities, 56, 95,
    116-117, 154, 156
Conflict resolution, 137, 153
  approach-approach, 138
  approach-avoidance, 139
  avoidance-avoidance,
      138-139